HOUSING, HERITAGE AND URBANISATION IN THE MIDDLE EAST AND NORTH AFRICA

Housing, Heritage and Urbanisation in the Middle East and North Africa

Edited by Lilia Makhloufi

OpenBook
Publishers

https://www.openbookpublishers.com

©2025 Lilia Makhloufi (ed.)
Copyright of individual chapters remains with the chapter's authors.

Paperback ISBN: 978-1-80511-561-8
Hardback ISBN: 978-1-80511-562-5
PDF ISBN: 978-1-80511-563-2
HTML ISBN: 978-1-80511-565-6
EPUB ISBN: 978-1-80511-564-9
DOI: 10.11647/OBP.0460

Cover image: Housing and local heritage in Algiers, Algeria. Photograph by Lilia Makhloufi (2020). All rights reserved.
Cover design: Jeevanjot Kaur Nagpal

Contents

Je dédie ce livre à mes parents,
pour m'avoir dirigé vers le monde académique et m'avoir encouragé à faire de
la recherche en dépit des difficultés rencontrées.
En retour, ils sont très satisfaits de me voir promue au titre de Professeur
depuis début 2025.

This publication is a result of the research project 'Housing Facing Metropolization: Innovative Approaches in Architecture and Urban Planning', conducted by Prof. Lilia Makhloufi and Prof. Dr. Ammar Abdulrahman, members of the Arab-German Young Academy of Sciences and Humanities (AGYA). The research project was funded by AGYA based in the Berlin-Brandenburg Academy of Sciences and Humanities (BBAW), Germany.

Disclaimer: The authors remain solely responsible for the content provided in this publication, which do not reflect the positions of AGYA or any of its funding partners.

aǧya

ARAB-GERMAN
YOUNG ACADEMY
OF SCIENCES AND
HUMANITIES

SPONSORED BY THE

Federal Ministry
of Education
and Research

Scientific and Review Committees

All chapters have been evaluated by an international scientific committee and an international review committee consisting of researchers from various academic backgrounds.

Scientific Coordinator and Chair of the Scientific and Review Committees

Prof. Lilia Makhloufi, Ecole Polytechnique d'Architecture et d'Urbanisme (EPAU), Algiers, Algeria. Alumna of the Arab-German Young Academy of Sciences and Humanities (AGYA), Berlin, Germany.

Scientific Committee Members

Prof. Lalla Btissam Drissi, LPHE-Modeling and Simulations, Faculty of Science, Mohammed V University, Rabat, Morocco (AGYA Alumna).

Prof. Ahmad Sakhrieh, Mechanical and Industrial Engineering Department, School of Engineering, American University of Ras Al Khaimah, 10021, United Arab Emirates. Mechanical Engineering Department, the University of Jordan, Amman 11942, Jordan (AGYA Alumnus).

Dr. Alaa Aldin Alchomari, Islamische Abteilung an der Uni Tübingen, Tübingen, Germany.

Dr. Honey Fadaie, Department of Architecture, Faculty of Art and Architecture, Roudehen Branch, Islamic Azad University (RIAU), Roudehen, Tehran, Iran.

Dr. Fanny Gerbeaud, Higher National School of Architecture and Landscape Architecture (ENSAP), Bordeaux, France. PAVE Research Centre, Bordeaux, France.

Dr. Ikram Hili, University of Sousse, Tunisia (AGYA Alumna).

Dr. Nibal Muhesen, cultural heritage expert at the Directorate General of Antiquities and Museums (DGAM), Damascus, Syria, and researcher at the University of Copenhagen, Denmark.

Review Committee Members

Prof. Khalid El Harrouni, Ecole Nationale d'Architecture, Rabat, Morocco.

Prof. Assia Lamzah, Institut National d'Aménagement et d'Urbanisme, Rabat, Morocco.

Dr. Ammar Abdulrahman, Institute for Ancient Near Eastern Studies of the Freie Universität Berlin, Germany (AGYA Alumnus).

Dr. Safa Achour, National School of Architecture and Urbanism of Tunis, Tunisia.

Dr. Carmen Antuña Rozado, Senior Scientist, MSc (Arch), VTT Technical Research Centre of Finland, Helsinki, Finland.

Dr. Aline Barlet, Higher National School of Architecture and Landscape Architecture (ENSAP), Bordeaux, France.

Dr. Honey Fadaie, Department of Architecture, Faculty of Art and Architecture, Roudehen Branch, Islamic Azad University (RIAU), Roudehen, Tehran, Iran.

Dr. Fanny Gerbeaud, Higher National School of Architecture and Landscape Architecture (ENSAP), Bordeaux, France. PAVE Research Centre, Bordeaux, France.

Dr. Nibal Muhesen, cultural heritage expert at the Directorate General of Antiquities and Museums (DGAM), Damascus, Syria, and researcher at the University of Copenhagen, Denmark.

Ms. Maryam Mirzaeii, Department of Architecture, Faculty of Art and Architecture, Roudehen Branch, Islamic Azad University (RIAU), Roudehen, Tehran, Iran.

Notes on Contributors

Asmaa Abdelhalim is an urban sociologist. She earned her bachelor's degree in architecture from Alexandria University's Faculty of Fine Arts in 2016, and a master's degree in urban development from Berlin Technical University in 2021, supported by scholarships from the German Academic Exchange Service (DAAD) and Sawiris Foundation for Sustainable Development in Egypt. She has worked on community driven development projects for Egyptian startups in old Cairo and the Blue Hole in South Sinai. In addition to community-based development, her interests include neighbourhood management and place-making.

ORCID ID: 0009-0008-6025-9408

Yossr Abouelnour is an architect, urban designer and researcher based in Berlin, currently pursuing an urban management degree at Berlin Technical University. She holds a master's degree in urban design from the University of Toronto and a bachelor's degree in architectural engineering from Ajman University. Her professional experience includes lecturing at the University of Science and Technology of Fujairah, working as a teaching and lab assistant at the University of Toronto and Ajman University, as well as practicing architecture, urban design and planning in the private sector for firms in Dubai, Romania and Toronto.

ORCID ID: 0009-0006-2598-5581

Nezha Alaoui obtained a PhD from the National School of Architecture of Rabat in 2022, and has held numerous professorships at both private and public universities. After earning her DENA architectural diploma in 2013, she founded the A.N. Architecture Agency. Her passion for her field has expanded within the office of renowned architect Zaha Hadid in London and the Atelier d'Urbanisme (APUR) in Paris. She has published numerous articles that have contributed to academic discourse in the fields of architecture, urban planning and design, and she has been invited by various public and private institutions to participate in and organise international symposiums and seminars. A passionate activist, she has spent years working to promote, protect and evaluate Moroccan heritage as a full member of the organisations Casa Mémoire and as a founding member of Rabat Salé Mémoire.

ORCID ID: 0009-0004-6230-1252

Athar Chabchoub is an architect pursuing an academic career path. After her master's degree, obtained with honors in 2013, she joined in the same year, the teaching staff of the National School of Architecture and Urbanism of Tunis (ENAU) in parallel with her research career as a doctoral student. Holding a doctoral degree in architectural sciences since 2019, her dissertation explores thermal comfort and its impact on the energy consumption of colonial and contemporary buildings in Tunis. She is currently engaged as a faculty lecturer, researcher and coordinator of the LaRPA research laboratory (PAE3C research team, ENAU).

ORCID ID: 0000-0002-9295-9731

Soufiane Essebbar is an architect and PhD candidate at the Centre of Doctoral Studies of the National School of Architecture in Morocco, where he obtained his DENA architectural diploma in 2015. As an architectural practitioner in the private sector, he has worked on numerous architectural and urban projects in national and international contexts, including France, the United Kingdom, Germany and the United Arab Emirates. His research interests include urban planning, architectural regulations and exploring interdisciplinary intersections between architecture, urban planning, history, politics and legal sciences.

ORCID ID: 0009-0008-6117-6532

Honey Fadaie is an assistant professor in the Department of Architecture at the Roudehen Branch of the Islamic Azad University in Iran, where she has taught as a board member for the past fifteen years. She has been studying Persian gardens since 2008, focusing on their sustainability and the traditional landscapes in hot and arid regions. Her current research interests include the concept of sustainability in Iranian tangible heritages.

ORCID ID: 0000-0003-4523-6028

Imane Fayyad has been an assistant at the University of Damascus since 2006. He pursued his master's degree in France in 2008, and in 2016, he defended his doctoral dissertation entitled 'The Domestic Habitat in Damascus, Homs and Hama of the Mamluk and Ottoman Periods (13th–18th Centuries)' at the University of Picardy in Amiens and at Ecole Pratique des Hautes Etudes (EPHE) in Paris. Several of his studies on these houses have since been published in peer-reviewed journals. Currently, he is an associate researcher at the TrAme laboratory (UR 4284) and the PROCLAC laboratory (UMR 7191) in France.

ORCID ID: 0009-0002-2050-687X

Fakher Kharrat is a professor of architecture specialising in the study and restoration of historical monuments and cultural heritage conservation. Formerly the director of the School of Architecture and Urbanism of Tunis and currently head of the Research Laboratory in Heritage and Architecturology (LaRPA), he has participated in various international projects related to architectural heritage as well as its conservation and enhancement.

ORCID ID: 0000-0002-1431-0523

Assia Lamzah is a trained architect and holds a PhD in landscape architecture from the University of Illinois at Urbana Champaign (UIUC), USA. She is currently a professor at Ecole Nationale d'Architecture (ENA), Rabat, Morocco. She has experience in teaching and research in architecture, urban and regional planning and landscape architecture. Her recent research projects focus on urban and architectural cultural heritage management, smart design, the relationship between architecture, landscape and social culture, and postcolonial theory.

ORCID ID: 0000-0002-1875-8632

Lilia Makhloufi is an architect and urban planner. She obtained her magister's degree in urban planning in 2003, and her doctorate of science degree in territory planning in 2009 and her postdoctoral degree (habilitation) with accreditation to supervise research in 2019. As a teacher and researcher, she worked at the University of Constantine, the University of Jijel and since 2010 at Ecole Polytechnique d'Architecture et d'Urbanisme (EPAU) in Algiers. In January 2025, she received a promotion to the rank of full professor of architecture.

She is also an Alumna of the Arab-German Young Academy of Sciences and Humanities (AGYA), based in the Berlin-Brandenburg Academy of Sciences and Humanities (BBAW) in Germany. Her main research experience and international collaborations are related to housing projects, public spaces, cities and sustainability.

ORCID ID: 0000-0002-8778-5132

Nibal Muhesen is a Syrian researcher in the field of archaeology and the protection of Syrian cultural heritage. He obtained a PhD from the University of Lyon II in Syrian archaeology in 2009. Since 2011, he has been involved in documenting the damage to Syrian cultural heritage and has participated in many international lectures and conferences aimed at protecting this heritage. He worked as an expert with the Syrian State Board of Antiquities where he took part in activities focusing on preserving and raising awareness about the importance of Syria's tangible and intangible heritage and advocating for community-driven reconstruction strategies. He is currently appointed to the Department of Tourism Management at the Faculty of Tourism at the University of Tartous as a researcher in the field of archaeology and tourism.

ORCID ID: 0009-0009-6050-5303

List of Illustrations

List of Tables

Preface

Lilia Makhloufi

This work is the outcome of an academic research project initiated and directed by Lilia Makhloufi under the title 'Housing Facing Metropolization: Innovative Approaches in Architecture and Urban Planning'.[1] The project was conducted under the sponsorship of the Arab-German Young Academy of Sciences and Humanities (AGYA) based in the Berlin-Brandenburg Academy of Sciences and Humanities (BBAW) in Germany.

This initiative was carried out in parallel to another academic research project, also funded by AGYA, titled 'Tangible and Intangible Heritage: Architecture, Design and Culture'.[2] This second project produced two distinct volumes:

- The first volume, *Tangible and Intangible Heritage in the Age of Globalisation*,[3] analysed and compared heritage in different contexts from an interdisciplinary perspective.

- The second volume, *Urban Heritage and Sustainability in the Age of Globalisation*, also presented a comparative and interdisciplinary analysis of heritage, but with an exclusive focus on the urban context.[4]

---

1   The project was conducted under grant 01DL20003 from the Federal Ministry of Education and Research (BMBF).
2   The project was also carried out under grant 01DL20003 from the BMBF.
3   Lilia Makhloufi (ed.), *Tangible and Intangible Heritage in the Age of Globalisation* (Cambridge, UK: Open Book Publishers, 2024), https://doi.org/10.11647/OBP.0388
4   Lilia Makhloufi (ed.), *Urban Heritage and Sustainability in the Age of Globalisation*. (Cambridge, UK: Open Book Publishers, 2024), https://doi.org/10.11647/OBP.0412

This third volume, *Housing, Heritage and Urbanisation in the Middle East and North Africa*, analyses housing in different urban contexts in the Middle East and North Africa from an interdisciplinary perspective. It includes the work of architects, archaeologists, urban sociologists, urban designers, urban planners and landscape architects. These PhD students, professors and practitioners from Algeria, Egypt, France, Germany, Iran, Morocco, Syria and Tunisia share the latest knowledge on both historic and new residential spaces in different urban contexts.

The scientific coordinator and the chair of the scientific and review committees would like to thank AGYA and the scientific committee members for their feedback on the submitted chapters during the review process, as well as the authors for their active contributions. Their engaging discussions, recommendations and debate on theoretical and practical approaches related to housing have been instrumental to the project's success.

Prof. Lilia Makhloufi
Scientific coordinator
Scientific and review committees Chair

Introduction

Housing and Local Heritage

Lilia Makhloufi

Local heritage, with its residential characteristics, is a source of architectural harmony, cultural identity, social unity and collective memory. As such, it holds immense significance for present and future generations. However, in recent years, local heritage has come under pressure due to global urban growth. In many cities, rapid development has led to a decline in the economic resources needed to improve residential buildings, basic facilities and infrastructure in older areas.

This book presents a comparative and interdisciplinary analysis of housing in the context of urbanisation, making a valuable contribution to the growing body of housing studies. The assessment analyses past and present residential spaces, examining (i) architectural and urban characteristics, (ii) social and cultural aspects, (iii) political and economic constraints and (iv) the role of the population in the transformation of old buildings.

The principles of standardisation promote uniformity in housing units through catering to common needs and adopting similar models of spatial organisation and universal construction standards. In response to this homogenisation, scholars have explored past and present conditions to foster sustainable housing development in cities around the globe.

Local heritage in general, especially its historic houses, reflects lifestyles of the past. These houses were designed according to the local context in which they were built, taking into account climatic conditions, landscape opportunities, topographical constraints,

  https://doi.org/10.11647/OBP.0460.00

existing construction materials and local customs and traditions. These parameters, fundamental to sustainable housing and urban planning, have provided long-term benefits for the well-being of local residents and must be preserved and passed on to future generations.

In this book, eleven researchers from various disciplines—including architecture, archaeology, urban sociology, urban design, urban planning and landscape architecture—share their approaches to housing, with perspectives on cities in the Middle East and North Africa. Considering this important topic from different angles, they enrich the debate on the past, present and future of housing in their respective countries and beyond.

Our collaborative work on this book has sparked an interdisciplinary exchange aimed at emphasising the multidimensional nature of housing and its intercultural potential. The contributors analyse local heritage, exploring residential features over time and considering the social and cultural characteristics that impact inhabitants. Across nine chapters, case studies are presented from Egypt, Iran, Morocco, Syria and Tunisia, structured according to the themes outlined below.

The first part of the book brings together archaeologists who share their perspectives on old cities and traditional housing in Syria. They examine the architectural and urban parameters of the past in order to improve those of the present and the future.

Chapter One examines the endangered vestiges of the Mamluk period in the old city of Damascus, focusing on the case of the al-Aglani and al-Tawil houses. Imane Fayyad richly illustrates and analyses this domestic architecture, including its building materials, spatial organisation and associated lifestyles. These Mamluk mansions represent a valuable yet little-known heritage of Damascus that should be preserved for present and future generations due to their historic, architectural and ornamental significance.

In Chapter Two, Nibal Muhesen considers the past in the context of the present, with a reflection on urban heritage destruction and housing in Syria. In this post-conflict society, heritage sites have come to accommodate communities, making this heritage an inseparable part of their everyday lives. Muhesen explores how this could encourage the restoration of damaged sites and the involvement of civil society in the process. She concludes that the reconstruction process should not be driven solely by economic circumstances or security concerns but should also enable social transformation and improve liveability in newly built environments.

The second part of the book brings together architects, urban planners and landscape architects who offer their perspectives on modern urban residential design. Reflecting on the Moroccan cities, these contributors approach urban processes and economic factors as intricately connected with social contexts.

Chapter Three considers housing and local identity through the prism of urban planning policy in Morocco. Soufiane Essebbar analyses the key factors that have influenced architecture and urban planning in the country, arguing that the methods borrowed from French urban planning have generated a crisis of identity, cultural expression and efficiency in Moroccan cities.

In Chapter Four, Nezha Alaoui addresses the design quality and sustainability of urban residential areas in Morocco, focusing on the legacy of colonial heritage in the metropolis of Casablanca. She reflects on the evolution of plans and facades over time, analysing the internal and external modification of modern housing to meet the cultural needs of local populations in three important districts. Her analysis investigates the relevance of these transformations and their impact on families and local communities.

Chapter Five examines Marrakesh medina in Morocco and how its colonial past has defined its contemporary perception. Assia Lamzah explores postcolonial issues related to the conception and reception of the medina. Her findings reveal that while the government and local decision-makers use cultural heritage to shape national identity, either in favour or in contrast to the colonial legacy, nonofficial users continue to perceive the medina as the backdrop of their everyday lives—a place of residence, work and leisure.

The third part of the book brings together urban designers and urban sociologists with perspectives on contemporary cities and residential identities in Egypt. Specifically, they highlight the cases of Cairo and Alexandria, two rapidly urbanising metropolises facing a variety of challenges related to urban transformation and housing issues.

In Chapter Six, Yossr Abouelnour examines the urban identity of a polarised metropolis, evaluating the strengths and weaknesses of informal settlements and gated communities in the Greater Cairo Area. She juxtaposes and compares the planning methods adopted in these communities, illustrating how liveable environments can be fostered by maximising community potential and strengthening inhabitants' sense of identity. Additionally, she questions the premise of a significant planning dichotomy between the two urban systems, their spatial configurations, and the opportunities they provide for their inhabitants.

Chapter Seven analyses the case of a fishermen village undergoing relocation as part of an urban renewal project. Asmaa Abdelhalim assesses the social effects of relocating the fishing community of El-Mex in Alexandria. The results of her post-relocation socio-economic study reveal that the relocated inhabitants suffer from high levels of grief, and some have since abandoned their fishing activities. However, she notes that relocation was not the sole cause of these socio-economic changes, identifying other factors such as the design of the new housing and dock and the change in economic status.

The fourth and final part of the book brings together architects who share their perspectives on the residential facades of metropolitan cities in Iran and Tunisia. These contributors view the challenge of achieving sustainable housing as a technical as well as cultural issue.

In Chapter Eight, Honey Fadaie examines the facade designs of residential buildings in metropolitan Tehran through the lens of traditional Iranian architectural principles. After identifying the main characteristics of Iranian facades, she analyses the design of selected buildings, evaluating the strategies of municipal committees tasked with aligning these facades with identity and climatic considerations. Based on this analysis, she then presents the most successful criteria and outcomes across Tehran's twenty-two districts.

Chapter Nine focuses on the facade of a contemporary building in the metropolis of Tunis, analysing its design approach and suitability for the Mediterranean climate. Athar Chabchoub assesses the impact of the building envelope on indoor thermal comfort during the summer, revealing weaknesses in the thermal performance of such buildings during hot seasons. This is followed by a parametric study that highlights the regulatory potential of envelopes with high thermal inertia for maintaining indoor thermal comfort and recommendations for optimising the thermal performance of contemporary buildings in Tunis.

Evaluating the chapters of this book from a comparative perspective reveals a series of insights into architectural and urban theories and practices in the Middle East and North Africa. The value of these insights is further enriched by the diverse national contexts represented by the constituent cases.

In Syria, several key cities such as Damascus, Aleppo and Homs have seen the destruction of their rich and diverse urban heritage fabric. This had led to the proliferation of irregular housing, constructed out of urgency during and after the conflict to accommodate displaced communities.

In Morocco, modern dwellings built during the period of French colonialism have undergone profound conceptual changes by their inhabitants. These modifications have resulted in hybrid dwellings that express cross-cultural ways of life, blending traditional Arab customs and European living standards.

In Egypt, the standardisation of residential spaces has produced stereotypical architectural and urban forms that fail to represent local identity or meet the specific social, cultural and spatial needs of today's population.

In both the Middle East and North Africa, architects often prioritise facade design in residential buildings to the detriment of thermal quality and climate adaptation. This is evident in the cases of Iran and Tunisia, where effective climate control is essential, especially during hot seasons.

Rather than focusing on the broader concept of urbanisation and its architectural and urban specificities, the contributors to this volume emphasise common approaches to solving issues related to residential heritage conservation. This approach sheds light on the local character of residential spaces, as well as the roles of inhabitants and public and private stakeholders in the urban transformation process.

The methodologies adopted in these chapters are particularly valuable for housing studies, as they offer salient insights into crucial urban, architectural and cultural aspects of the Middle East and North Africa and their influence on residential spaces, both historically and in contemporary contexts. For instance, comparative studies are shown to be an efficient tool in urban development processes and architectural heritage conservation, while social surveys offer alternative approaches to sustainable housing and residential management.

Moreover, the contributors identify common threats and limitations related to the aesthetics and sustainability of modern and contemporary cities. The global spread of the international style, for example, has led to the homogenisation of facade designs worldwide. This standardisation in contemporary architecture has significant implications for the environmental quality of residential buildings and the well-being of their inhabitants.

Throughout history, human beings have proven adept at adapting architecture to local climates, resulting in homes tailored to specific living environments. Residential building designs that do not take climatic factors into account will inevitably fail to meet the thermal comfort needs of inhabitants.

Reflecting on the historical, social and political contexts of formerly colonised cities in North Africa and the Middle East, their contemporary conception appears multifaceted and controversial. Here, the cultural dimension extends beyond architectural and urban features, emphasising inhabitant comfort as an essential consideration in reaching viable solutions.

Today, urban identity and social ties play a major role in community cohesion within newly built residential areas, grounded in shared values, collective norms and similar ways of life. Therefore, the process of residents' appropriation of space is closely connected to identities, lifestyles and social structures in modern cities and metropolises. Moreover, design approaches that align with the principles of Mediterranean architecture improve the well-being of the local population.

Consequently, a long-term perspective is crucial in considering the actions of local decision-makers, architects and urban planners. The full involvement of civil society in the preservation of local knowledge and expertise is likewise more imperative than ever.

The contributors to this volume have come together from various disciplines to share the latest knowledge on residential spaces in selected cities and countries in the Middle East and North Africa. Their research highlights unique architectural and urban features, locations, climatic conditions and local commitment to heritage preservation and maintenance.

The completion of this book faced significant challenges, as it was undertaken during the COVID-19 pandemic. This necessitated that the entire editorial process be conducted by email, with contributors living in different countries and time zones. Despite these obstacles, the diverse yet complementary research on housing presented in this book makes a valuable contribution to the promotion of local heritage, socio-cultural aspirations and the well-being of contemporary urban populations. We hope that these insights will have a positive impact on the readership of Open Book Publishers.

I. OLD CITIES AND TRADITIONAL HOUSING IN SYRIA

1. Endangered Residential Vestiges of the Mamluk Period in the Old City of Damascus: The Case of the al-Aglani and al-Tawil Houses

Imane Fayyad

Introduction

For decades, the study of the architecture of the Islamic world has largely been limited to religious edifices like mosques, *madrasas* [schools] and mausoleums, occasionally extending to include palatial structures. Residential architecture, by contrast, has been relegated to a secondary status, as a result of several factors. Houses not lost to the ravages of time are often in disrepair, or else their occupants may oppose the study of them. Moreover, mention of these structures in scholarly sources is very often scarce.

The architectural heritage from the Mamluk period (1250–1516) is a notable example. Poorly preserved and generally little-known, this heritage is now threatened not only by the ongoing war in Syria but also by the absence of a heritage authority to safeguard against destruction in these tumultuous times. This research focuses on the historical, architectural and decorative analysis of Mamluk mansions in Damascus, drawing from the examples of the al-Aglani and al-Tawil houses to

https://doi.org/10.11647/OBP.0460.01

uncover the principles of Mamluk architecture, including building materials, domestic space organisation and lifestyles.

The Mamluks were originally slaves captured from Kipchaq in Central Asia, after which they underwent military training and were introduced to Islam.[1] In this historical context, the Arabic word 'Mamluk', meaning 'owned', denotes a foreign military slave acquired to serve as an elite fighter under the direct authority of the sultan.

Entering the service of the Ayyubid princes (1175–1260), the Mamluks soon gained substantial power. Taking advantage of inefficiency and division among their masters during the Crusades and Mongolian threats, the Mamluks were eventually able to seize power and establish the Mamluk Sultanate, which ruled as one of the major Islamic powers for nearly three hundred years.[2]

They soon extended their empire to Egypt, Palestine and Syria as well as to the holy cities of Hejaz, reigning with absolute authority until 1517. However, Mamluk dominance began to decline with the opening of European trade routes through the Cape of Good Hope, and their reign was ultimately extinguished by Ottoman expansion in the early sixteenth century.[3]

The number of studies on traditional housing in regions like the Mediterranean has multiplied in recent years. Although in cities like Cairo and Tunis large houses have been studied extensively, the same attention has not been given to Syria, despite its exceptional heritage. Research on residences in the Syrian capital of Damascus is scarce and often cursory, prompting the need for a twofold analysis encompassing both the medieval origins and the subsequent transformation of this urban space.

Focusing on Mamluk residential remnants, this study aims to contribute to the documentation of Damascene urban domestic heritage through the creation of archives showcasing the originality of

---

1   David Ayalon, 'The Muslim City and the Mamluk Military Aristocracy', in Ayalon, *Studies on the Mamluks of Egypt 1250–1517* (London: Variorum Reprints, 1977), pp. 311–29.

2   Jean-Claude Garcin, 'Le système militaire mamluk et le blocage de la société musulmane médiévale', *AnIsl*, 24 (1988), 93–94.

3   Julien Loiseau, *Les Mamelouks (XIIIᵉ-XVIᵉ siècle). Une expérience du pouvoir dans l'islam médiéval* (Paris: Editions du Seuil, 2014), pp. 41–42.

these endangered buildings. This research builds on archival records from the Directorate General of Antiquities and Museums (DGAM), Syria, adjusting many of the plans and elevations with the assistance of Damascus architect Mr. Hussam Ahmad. Cases comprising plans, sections and photographs were compiled using AutoCAD software, representing the first such architectural examination of these buildings. In order to identify the specific characteristics of the Mamluk domestic heritage in Damascus, two examples were selected: the al-Aglani and al-Tawil houses, located in the immediate vicinity of the Umayyad Mosque.

In terms of spatial organisation, typical houses from this period in Damascus feature an open inner courtyard surrounded by habitable rooms and service areas such as kitchens and cellars. This layout is common to both affluent and modest households. The Mamluk architectural style is characterised by distinctive facades utilising two-tone *ablaq* in the building foundations, as observed in the al-Aglani and al-Tawil houses, along with the use of polychrome marble embellished with coloured paste.

Many old houses in Damascus remain inhabited and have undergone several transformations over time. The overcrowding of residences, with multiple families often inhabiting a single dwelling, has led to alterations in spatial structure and function. Additionally, modern comforts such as kitchen and bathroom renovations and reorganisation of room layouts to circumvent courtyards in the winter are common adaptations. These transformations can be seen in both the al-Aglani and al-Tawil residences.

The first challenge to arise during this research was the absence of early historical records, which are unavailable from either the City Hall or DGAM. Additionally, the houses have undergone alterations due to the fragility and deterioration of the original building materials. These necessary renovations have made it difficult to ascertain the residential characteristics of houses from the Mamluk period or the Mamluk-Ottoman transition of the sixteenth century.

Dating the structures accurately poses an additional methodological challenge. In the absence of explicitly dated elements, a comparative method was used based on well-dated historic public buildings such as *madrasas* and mosques. Comparisons and cross-checking allowed for the formulation of assumptions, with the al-Aqqad residence serving as a reference point for approximate dating due to its satisfactory historical documentation and state of repair. This house, currently situated on cadastral parcel n° 976, is notable for its unique lower-storey vestiges, which likely date back to the fifteenth and sixteenth centuries.[4] Below, the locations of the selected houses are presented on a map of the old city of Damascus (Figure 1.1).

al-Saqqa Amini house

al-Aglani house

al-Saqqa Amini house

al-Aqqad house

Fig. 1.1 Map of old Damascus marking the locations of the selected houses. Author's illustration, CC BY-NC-ND.

The al-Aglani House

History and Location

Several theories have been offered concerning the history of the al-Aglani house. Carl Watzinger and Karl Wulzinger suggested it

---

4   Steven Weber and Peder Mortensen, 'The Bayt al-Aqqad between the 15th and the 18th Century', in *Proceedings of the Danish Institute in Damascus, IV, Bait al-Aqqad. The History and Restoration of a House in old Damascus*, ed. by Peder Mortensen (Aarhus: Aarhus University Press, 2005), pp. 227–79 (p. 228).

was originally the home of the Caliph Yazid, son of Muawiya.[5] In the fifteenth century, it became a Mamluk palace under the ownership of the Banu Mangak family, after which it was known as Ṣarim al-Din Ibn Mangak House.[6]

In a 2013 article, Elodie Vigouroux identifies Emir Ibrahim Ibn Mangak as another owner of the house, drawing on two historical testimonies. According to the first, from Ibn Tulan, Mangak owned a house built on the site of Hammam al-Sahn, but it was destroyed in the late fourteenth century and remained derelict until at least 1413.[7] The second account, that of Ibn al-Himsi, speaks of Mangak's construction of the house over the ruins of the Umayyad Mosque, stating that it was burned by Tamerlan in 1401. Vigouroux also indicates that the house was named after the prominent Ottoman al-Aglani family following their intermarriage with the Mangaks.

Located east of the Umayyad Mosque, the al-Agani House has recently been converted into a commercial property. It currently occupies three parcels of land in the al-Amarah al-Gawwaniyya/Bab al-Barid District. This includes parcel n°162, which contains the largest concentration of ruins and is thus the focus of this research. The only detailed study of the al-Aglani residence was conducted by Riham al-Hagg during his restoration of the house in 2014.[8] The present research draws upon the author's 2011 survey of the oldest part of the house. This structure now consists of three storeys, of which only the ground floor is relevant to the present study. Here, two features are especially noteworthy: the exterior northern facade, with a large portal overlooking the street, and the interior southern facade (Figure 1.2).

---

5   Carl Watzinger and Karl Wulzinger, *Damaskus die Islamische Stadt*, 2 vols, 2nd edn ([Berlin and Leipzig] Damascus: Walter de Gruyter & Co, [1924] 1984), II, 66.

6   Elodie Vigouroux, *Damas après Tamerlan étude historique et archéologique d'une renaissance (1401–1481)* (Paris: Université Paris-Sorbonne, 2011), p. 63.

7   Elodie Vigouroux, 'Les Banu Mangak à Damas. Capital social, enracinement local et gestion patrimoniale d'une famille d'*awlad al-nas* à l'époque mamelouke', *AnIsI*, 47 (2013), 197–233 (pp. 205–06).

8   Riham al-Hagg, *Masaru Dar al-Aglani* (Damascus: University of Damascus, 2014), pp. 11–12.

The portal

The court

qā'a

Re-added Mamluk Remains

al-Aglani house

0   1   5м

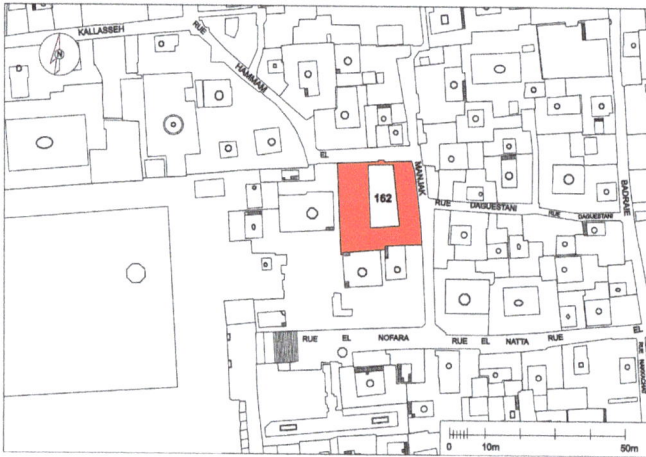

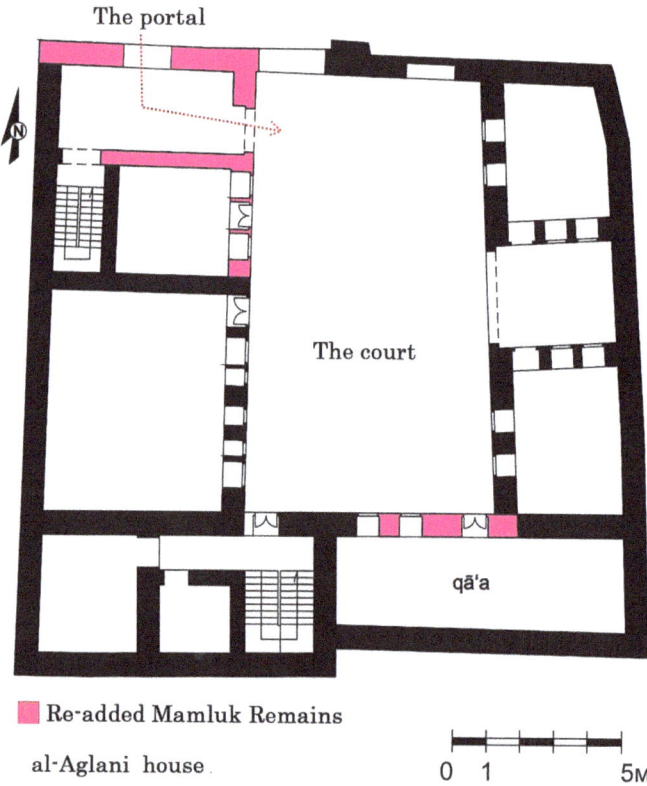

Fig. 1.2 The al-Aglani House: cadastral plan showing the house and ground floor plan. Author's illustration, CC BY-NC-ND.

The Northern Facade and Portal

The house's northern facade rests atop what appears to be repurposed Roman foundations. The uneven rubble stones, measuring approximately 0.70 metres in size, are similar to those observed in the al-Aqqad house. The foundations consist of irregular stones approximately 0.27 metres high, constructed of cut stones of basalt and limestone and reaching a height of approximately 1.60 meters. The foundations of buildings constructed in Damascus during the fifteenth and early sixteenth centuries typically average around 0.30 metres in depth, while during the seventeenth and eighteenth centuries, the average depth was reduced to approximately 0.22 metres. With few exceptions to this rule, the majority of Damascene structures with foundations measuring less than 0.30 metres can be confidently dated back to this period.[9]

The rest of the facade has been recently redesigned (Figure 1.3). In the centre, a porch terminating in a tri-lobed arch spans the height of the facade. Within this porch, a 0.30 metre recess accommodates a large slightly pointed arched portal enclosing a smaller door known as a *huha*. This typical feature of al-Saqqa Amini homes allows for convenient access without the need to open the main door.

Preserving elements of its original construction, the house features a courtyard with two noteworthy facades to the south and north. The walls of these facades are adorned with geometric panels likely dating back to the Mamluk period in the fourteenth and fifteenth centuries (Figure 1.4).[10]

---

9   Marianne Boqvist, 'Building Materials and Construction Techniques', in *Proceedings of the Danish Institute in Damascus, IV, Bait al-Aqqad. The History and Restoration of a House in old Damascus*, ed. by Peder Mortensen (Aarhus: Aarhus University Press, 2005), pp. 129–39 (p. 135).

10   Imane Fayyad, *L'habitat domestique à Damas, Homs et Hama aux époques mamelouke et ottomane (XIIIᵉ-XVIIIᵉ siècle)* (Paris: Ecole Pratique des Hautes Etudes, 2016), p. 131.

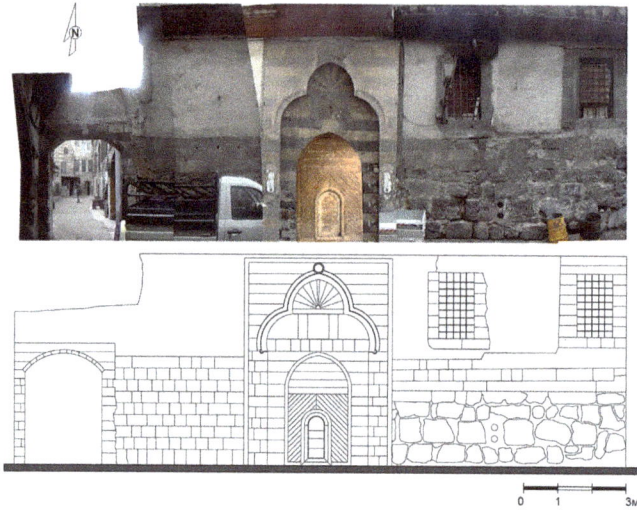

Fig. 1.3 The al-Aglani house: elevation of the exterior north facade. Author's photograph and illustration, 2012, CC BY-NC-ND.

al-Saqqa Amini house   al-Aglani house

Fig. 1.4 Two examples of portals with *huha*. Author's photographs and illustrations, 2012, CC BY-NC-ND.

Above the portal, the wall consists of alternating *ablaq* rows, which scholars suggest also date back to the Mamluk period.[11] This design resembles the northern facade of the al-Aqqad house as well as another house in the Qabr Atika District. At the end of the portal, a square panel connected to the porch frame by a decorative buckle features geometric black and white stars topped by a semicircle embellished with black and white rays. This opening duplicates the gate and may have allowed guests to enter the building without disrupting the privacy of family life. The eastern end of the facade consists of a low arch leading to a courtyard, constructed with reused *ablaq* stones partially adorned with rosettes. Inside the courtyard, remnants of a fountain can be found in a shallow niche with a slightly arched top decorated with *ablaq*. In the rear is a square panel embellished with stars and geometric patterns similar to those of the porch. The presence of the fountain testifies to the house's importance, raising questions as to whether it served as a water supply source for the family and whether it was accessible to the local public. Watzinger and Wulzinger date its origins back to the Mamluk in the fifteenth century (Figure 1.5).[12]

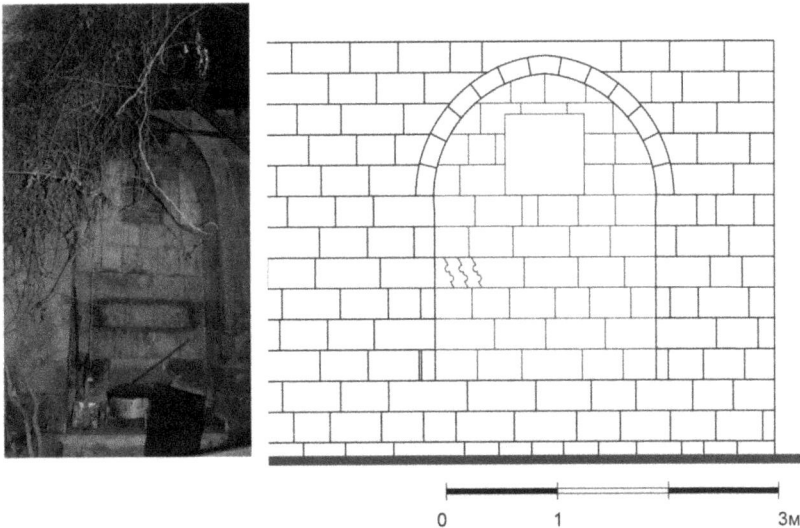

Fig. 1.5 The al-Aglani house: elevation of the fountain of the north interior facade. Author's photograph and illustration, 2012, CC BY-NC-ND.

---

11   Boqvist, 'Building Materials and Construction Techniques', p. 135.
12   Watzinger and Wulzinger, *Damaskus die Islamische Stadt*, II, 66.

In contrast to the right half of the facade, which was redesigned during the eighteenth and nineteenth centuries save for a single door framed by an *ablaq* pattern, the left half of the facade is more significant and well preserved. Facing north, this section features five windows positioned to the right of a door topped by two rectangular windows, separated from the upper level by two ornamental wave friezes. These two windows are framed by slightly pointed arches, between which is a circular panel with predominantly geometric ornaments. Two bands, one of *ablaq* and the other of carved limestone, underly each window. Two framing strips are connected to the top of the arches by a buckle of carved limestone. The western end resembles the facade of the al-Saqifa Mosque, suggesting it dates back to the Mamluk period (Figure 1.6). The lower part of the wall is made up of a number of decorated carved stones, which have been repurposed and are likely of Mamluk origin. Two rectangular windows with a falling arch lintel can also be dated to the Mamluk period (Figure 1.7).

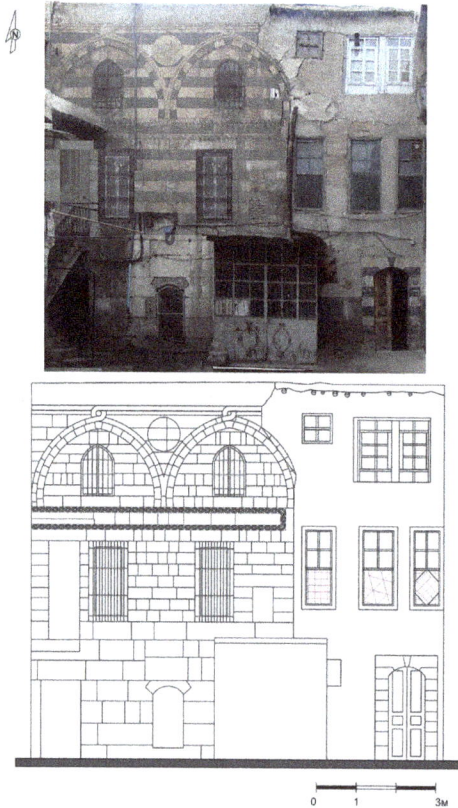

Fig. 1.6 The al-Aglani house: elevation of the interior south facade. Author's photograph and illustration, 2012, CC BY-NC-ND.

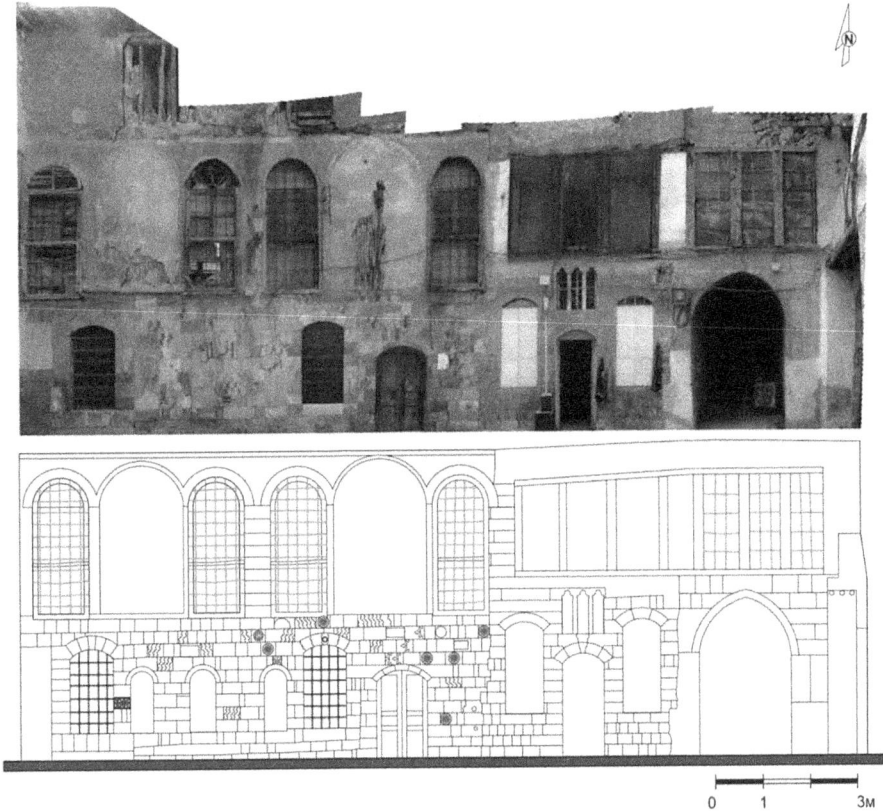

Fig. 1.7 The al-Aglani house: elevation of the interior eastern facade. Author's photograph and illustration, 2012, CC BY-NC-ND.

The al-Tawil House

History and Location

The architectural style of the al-Tawil residence is representative of the traditional Damascene house, evolving from the sixteenth century until the late Ottoman period in the eighteenth century. According to extracts from the land register of the old city of Damascus, the house was renovated in 1840, introducing the European architectural influence of the French rococo and Italian baroque styles.

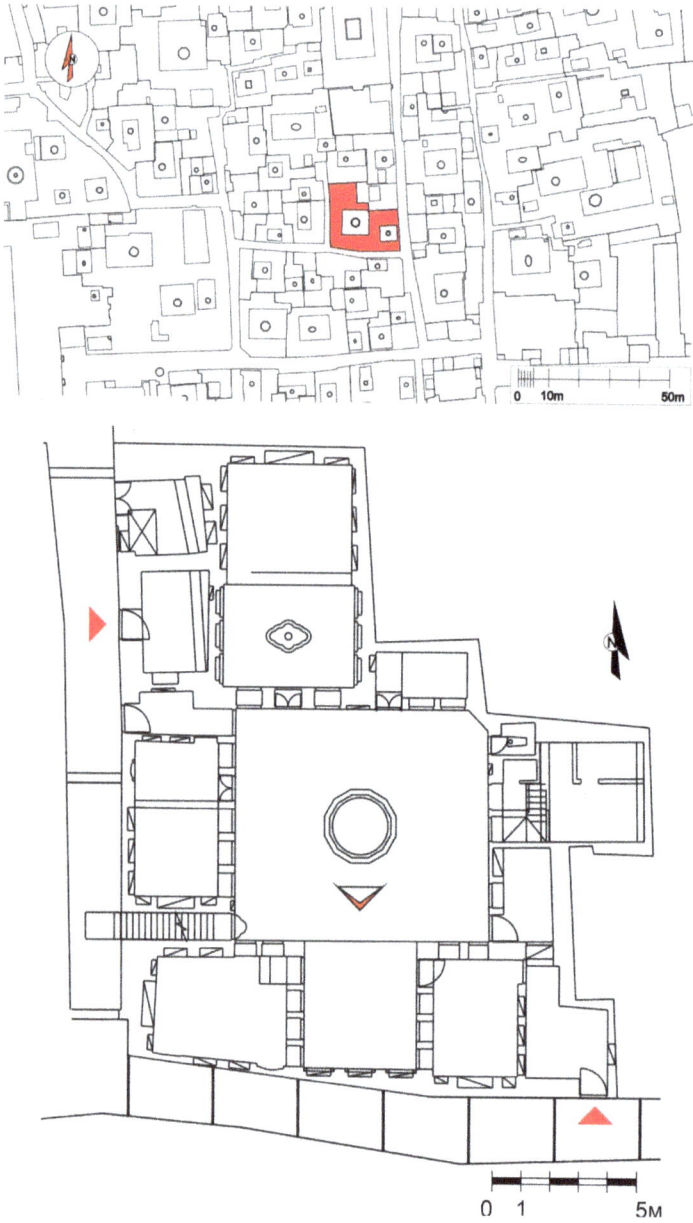

Fig. 1.8 The al-Tawil house: cadastral plan situating the house and plan of the ground floor. Illustration by Mohammad Daruis and the author, 2012, CC BY-NC-ND.

Despite retaining much of its historical character, the al-Tawil residence has not been subject to extensive study, save for during a 2009 restoration project by architect Mohammad Darius.[13] In 2012, an archaeological survey was conducted by the author on the house's oldest segment. Located in the heart of the old city, east of the Great Umayyad Mosque, the house belongs to the al-Tawil family. It is currently registered under parcel n°279-2, al-Amarah al-Gawwaniyya. The north side of the house faces the main street leading toward Nafura, while the south side borders Dagstani Alley. There are two covered entries to the house, one on its west facade in a recess formed by Dagstani Alley, and one on its south facade.

According to the 1934 cadastral plan of the old city, the house was divided into three independent residences. The structure consists of two storeys, covering an area of 310.04 square metres. The ground floor included an inner courtyard, an *iwan*,[14] a kitchen, a small cellar, reception or living areas (*qa'a*), and utility rooms. Upstairs, there were six living rooms (Figure 1.8).

Every entrance to the house leads through a rectangular courtyard enclosing an octagonal stone pool. Four *qa'a*, or reception rooms, are arranged around the courtyard: two on the south side beside the *iwan*, and three facing each other on the north, west and east sides. These rooms traditionally vary in dimension and location, and although their use is subject to speculation, the abundant ornamentation suggests they were likely reception spaces. However, this applies only to those located on the ground floor. Now we turn to the element of greatest interest to this study: the *iwan*, on the southern side of the courtyard, which contains the oldest likely remnants of the sixteenth-century Mamluk period.

The *Iwan*

Part of the main facade of the house, the *iwan* is a three-walled rectangular chamber measuring 4.23 metres wide and 7.82 metres high.

---

13   Mohammad Daruis, *Tautiq wa Tarmim Bayt al-Tawil- al-Amarah al-Gawwaniyya-Dimasq al-Qadimah* (Damascus: University of Damascus, 2009), pp. 41–42.

14   It is a room made up of three walls, the fourth opening through a large arch onto the interior courtyard (Fayyad, *L'habitat domestique à Damas*, p. 335).

Constructed with white and black stones, it is crowned by a white limestone pediment with a cornice adorned with decorative stylised geometric shapes. A similar white limestone cornice runs along the entire length of the facade. Frames featuring this same pattern can be found on other sixteenth-century buildings including the al-Aqqad house, completed in 1526.[15]

The *iwan* is a room opening into the courtyard, facing entirely north on account of a slightly dropped arch made of two-tone white and black keystones. These prominent limestone patterns encroach upon the stone ornaments of the arch moulding.

The *ablaq* technique was used for both the top and bottom of the arch, typical of sixteenth-century architecture. Its voussoirs are adorned with two successive friezes of eight-pointed stars, a pattern which also appears in the intrados, complemented by stylised coloured rosettes in coloured paste. The arch supports are made of decorated calcareous stones, as in al-Aqqad house. The ceiling is simple, comprising an arrangement of wooden beams. Within the *iwan*, three recesses are featured on each wall, along with two smaller niches in the back wall. The lowered arch lintels are inlaid with rosettes and topped by panels embellished in the European French rococo and Italian baroque styles (Figure 1.9).

Adjacent to the courtyard, the first room west of the *iwan* is accessed through a door surrounded by a rectangular frame with a broken arch, the lintel of which is decorated at its centre with a white, red and black geometric pattern made of coloured paste. This rectangular room may have been used as a living room.

No traces of older decoration are visible alongside the aforementioned European-style decorative elements. Several *kutbiyya*, a kind of open cupboard with two shelves for exhibiting valuable items, line the walls, extending to the height of the windowsills. The second room, east of the *iwan*, features a door and three windows opening onto the *iwan*. However, assumptions about the floor and ceiling coatings cannot be made with certainty, and the current flooring has a modern coating.

---

15   Daruis, *Tautiq wa Tarmim Bayt*, pp. 41–42.

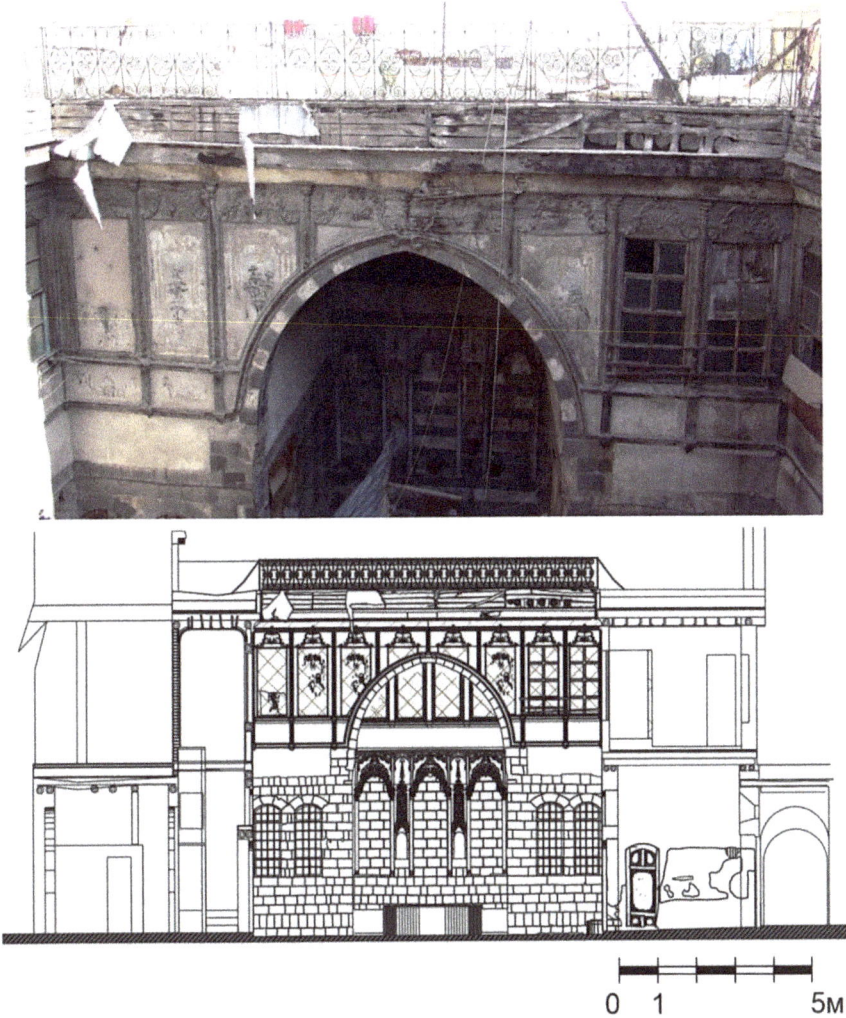

Fig. 1.9 The al-Tawil house: view of the south facade (*iwan*) and its arch. Author's photograph and illustration, 2012, CC BY-NC-ND.

Conclusion

This study has identified historical, architectural and decorative characteristics of Mamluk mansions in Damascus, focusing on the examples of the al-Aglani and al-Tawil houses. At the former, the height of the limestone and black basalt foundations as well as the northern and southern facades have been determined likely to date back to the Mamluk period in the fifteenth century, as they are markedly similar to the al-Aqqad house's northern facade. Furthermore, the initial construction elements of the al-Aglani reception rooms may also derive from this era, a claim supported by the resemblance of their brickwork to that of the fifteenth-century facade of Qabr Atika's house. The Nadir house, near the Tawrizi Mosque in the Sagur District has a facade likely dating to the end of the fifteenth century, which has similarities with the al-Tawil house.[16] According to the current owner, the richly decorated facade is that of the mausoleum of Abu Sufyan.[17] As we were unable to enter the house, we based our study of this facade on the photos taken by Steven Weber and Marianne Boqvist.[18]

On the basis of these historical elements, it is possible to identify certain consistent characteristics of Mamluk residential architecture in Damascus from the fifteenth and sixteenth centuries, in terms of construction, spatial organisation and ornamentation. The predominant building materials include limestone for bedrocks, door/window frames, baked clay for the upper sections of walls, lime for wall coating and painted wood for ceilings. Building techniques typically involve horizontal layers of medium-sized cut stone and wood quoins filled with mortar (mud bricks) for wall construction. Ceilings feature alternating beams and cob.

The present chapter has included only two houses as samples from a wider body of research on residential architecture in Damascus. Thus, the continuation of this research will entail expanding the scope of the study to include residences in various neighbourhoods of old Damascus, with the prospect of establishing a comprehensive typology of these houses.

---

16   Boqvist, 'Building Materials and Construction Techniques', p. 135.
17   Weber and Mortensen, 'The Bayt al-Aqqad', pp. 234–35.
18   For more about this facade, see Fayyad, *L'habitat domestique à Damas*, p. 79 and figures 85–86.

Bibliography

al-Hagg, Riham, *Masaru Dar al-Aglani* (Damascus: University of Damascus, 2014).

Ayalon, David, 'The Muslim City and the Mamluk Military Aristocracy', in Ayalon, *Studies on the Mamluks of Egypt 1250–1517* (Lonedon: Variorum Reprints, 1977).

Boqvist, Marianne, 'Building Materials and Construction Techniques', in *Proceedings of the Danish Institute in Damascus, IV, Bait al-Aqqad. The History and Restoration of a House in Old Damascus*, ed. by Peder Mortensen (Aarhus: Aarhus University Press 2005), pp. 129–39.

Daruis, Mohammad, *Tautiq wa Tarmim Bayt al-Tawil- al-Amarah al-Gawwaniyya-Dimasq al-Qadimah* (Damascus: University of Damascus, 2009).

Fayyad, Imane, *L'habitat domestique à Damas, Homs et Hama aux époques mamelouke et ottomane (XIIIᵉ-XVIIIᵉ siècle)* (Paris: Ecole Pratique des Hautes Etudes, 2016).

Garcin, Jean-Claude, 'Le système militaire mamluk et le blocage de la société musulmane médiévale', *AnIsl*, 24 (1988), 93–94.

Loiseau, Julien, *Les Mamelouks (XIIIᵉ-XVIᵉ siècle). Une expérience du pouvoir dans l'islam médiéval* (Paris: Editions du Seuil, 2014).

Vigouroux, Elodie, *Damas après Tamerlan étude historique et archéologique d'une renaissance (1401–1481)* (Paris: Université Paris-Sorbonne, 2011).

Vigouroux, Elodie, 'Les Banu Mangak à Damas. Capital social, enracinement local et gestion patrimoniale d'une famille d'*awlad al-nas* à l'époque mamelouke', *AnIsl*, 47 (2013), 197–233.

Watzinger, Carl and Wulzinger, Karl, *Damaskus die Islamische Stadt*, 2 vols, 2nd edn ([Berlin and Leipzig] Damascus: Walter de Gruyter & Co, [1924] 1984).

Weber, Steven and Mortensen, Peder, 'The Bayt al-Aqqad between the 15ᵗʰ and the 18ᵗʰ Century', in *Proceedings of the Danish Institute in Damascus, IV, Bait al-Aqqad. The History and Restoration of a House in Old Damascus*, ed. by Peder Mortensen (Aarhus: Aarhus University Press, 2005), pp. 227–79.

2. The Past in the Present: Urban Heritage Destruction and Housing in Syria

Nibal Muhesen[1]

Introduction

Cultural heritage, in both its tangible and intangible components, has suffered significant damage as a result of the war in Syria. Several key cities like Aleppo, Homs and Deir ez-Zor have seen the loss of the fabric of their rich and diverse urban heritage due not only to the war but also to the unavoidable reconstruction activities necessary to secure housing for people displaced by the conflict. State authorities faced the dual challenge of responding immediately to the population's escalating and urgent humanitarian needs, while also pursuing restoration plans in affected areas. Consequently, alongside official reconstruction initiatives, there has been a rise in unauthorised building activities in several Syrian cities, including in their archaeological areas. Desperate for shelter, people have reoccupied ancient sites as well as various new, unauthorised constructions and rubbish dumps, coinciding with the looting of archaeological sites such as the 'Dead Cities' and Bosra. The

---

1   The author would like to thank Dr. Ammar Abdulrahman and Dr. Lilia Makhloufi for extending this kind invitation to him and for their intellectual contribution to the debate about the topic of housing. He is also grateful to his colleagues in Syria and Denmark for their help.

     https://doi.org/10.11647/OBP.0460.02

exact extent of the resulting damage is still impossible to assess,[2] raising the question of what will remain of Syria's urban heritage after the complete cessation of hostilities on Syrian territory and the departure of all militant groups from the country. Additionally, it highlights the urgent need to rehouse displaced communities, sometimes at the expense of heritage protection.

This chapter sheds light on wartime urban heritage destruction as well as other conflict-related issues affecting urban heritage, including the use of heritage sites as shelters for shattered communities.[3] These issues have sparked heated debates on the nature and feasibility of restoring damaged sites in recent years. Against this backdrop, heritage has become an inseparable part of everyday life and a shelter or accommodation for affected inhabitants. Thus, reconstruction strategies should not reflect vital economic and security concerns alone but must also facilitate social transformation and improve the relationship between inhabitants and their new environment.

Urban Heritage Destruction

Though many of the concepts developed here focus on the destruction of cities in Syria, the larger framework of urban destruction should also be taken into account. In fact, across the Arabic region, several contemporary episodes of severe destruction have taken place, such as in Iraq (Mosul, Al Anbar), Yemen (Sanaa, Aden, Taiz) and Libya

---

2   Directorate General of Antiquities and Museums (DGAM), *Report on the State of Conservation of Syrian Cultural Heritage Sites* (Damascus: DGAM, 2021).

3   Local inhabitation of Syria's archaeological sites is not a strictly recent phenomenon. Before excavating Palmyra in the 1930s, French mandatory authorities had to evict locals from the Roman temples. Additionally, in the aftermath of the February 2023 earthquake in the region, reports from Idlib in north-western Syria documented local use of sites as shelters, agricultural lands or stone quarries, resulting in unauthorised constructions, site vandalism, and the inability to monitor procedures, including at the sites of al-Bara, Serjela and Saint Simeon Church. See Mathilde Gelin, *L'Archéologie en Syrie et au Liban à l'Epoque du Mandat 1919–1946* (Paris: Librairie Orientaliste, 2002); Isber Sabrine, Abdulhman Alyhia and Mahmoud Barkat, *The Impact of the 2023-Earthquake on Archaeological Locations in Northwest Syria* (n.p.: Heritage for Peace, 2023), https://ansch.heritageforpeace.org/wp-content/uploads/2023/03/the-impact-of-the-2023-earthquake-on-the-archaeological-locations-on-the-Syrian-coast.pdf

(Tripoli).[4] In all of these cases, there has been an annihilation of collective local urban identity. In fact, urban assaults are understood herein as the intentional annihilation of entire urban landscapes due to their cultural and social significance. Since ancient times, the destruction of cities has been used as a means of inflicting severe damage not only on tangible urban heritage but on collective identity, values and traditions.[5]

Destruction of Syrian Urban Heritage

The significant death-toll, involvement of multiple parties and widespread devastation in major Syrian cities qualifies the war as an armed and open international conflict.[6] Moreover, the devastation of the country's urban landscape amounts to the destruction of the population's traditions, values and ways of life within specific urban contexts.

Prior to the start of the conflict, Syrian cities were hubs of population concentration and various cultural and economic activities. There was an intense attachment to these cities among their inhabitants, with many Syrians identifying themselves by their native cities—for example, Šāmi (from Damascus) or ḥālābī (from Aleppo). Notably, these labels of self-identification still persist in the present context, with displaced communities continuing to identify with cities in which they are no longer physically present.

---

4   The concept of Urbicide, referring to the purposeful destruction of urban fabric, local identity and memory, is relevant to this research, and has been explored in various contexts including Beirut, Lebanon (1975–90) and Nablus, Palestine (2003–05). See Martin Coward, *Urbicide: The Politics of Urban Destruction* (New York: Routledge, 2009), pp. 186–89.

5   For instance the cities of Hama in modern Syria and Carthage in modern Tunisia. Catherine Sandes, 'Urban Cultural Heritage and Armed Conflict: The Case of Beirut Central District', in *Cultural Heritage in the Crosshairs: Protecting Cultural Property during Conflict*, ed. by Joris Kila and James Zeidler (Leiden: Brill, 2013), pp. 287–315.

6   Rogier Bartels, 'The Classification of Armed Conflicts by International Criminal Courts and Tribunals', *International Criminal Law Review*, 20 (2020), 595–668.

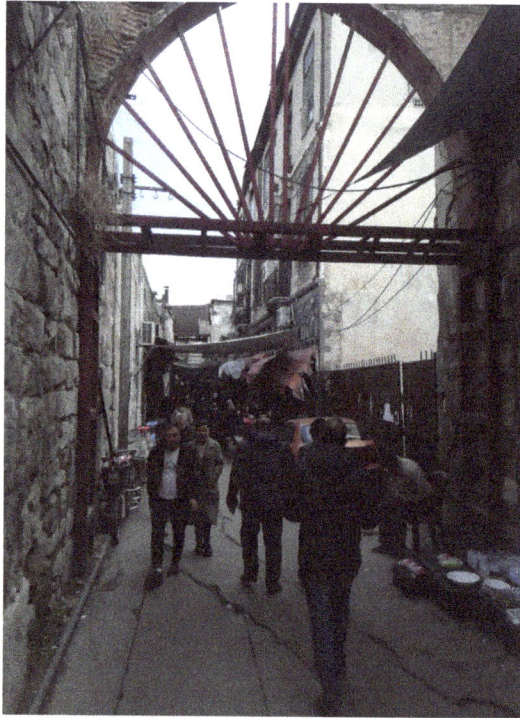

Fig. 2.1 View of the Old Town of Damascus, where modern metallic structures are used to consolidate the fragile historic buildings. Author's photograph, 2023, CC BY-NC-ND.

Additionally, it has been argued that the historic urban centres of Aleppo and Damascus have been deteriorating for the past two decades due to unchecked modernisation trends combined with ineffective approaches and policies related to tourism. Since the outbreak of the conflict in 2011–12, this deterioration has intensified, as urban infrastructure as well as monuments and heritage sites have sustained partial or total damage. This includes UNESCO World Heritage Sites such as the Ancient City of Aleppo or the Krak des Chevaliers in Homs.

Cultural heritage sites have been destroyed by fire as well as damaged beyond repair as a result of shelling and clashes. Between 2012 and 2016, during the height of the war, severe acts of destruction were committed by various parties. Thus, the Syrian conflict has entailed a significant urban warfare component, leading to wide-ranging alterations and destruction of the urban landscape in several cities, including densely populated Damascus (see Figure 2.1), Homs, Aleppo and Deir ez-Zor.

It should be emphasised that in the course of the present conflict, it has been difficult to determine whether urban destruction has been purposeful or has merely coincided with the major battles which have unfolded in Syrian towns and cities.[7] This requires an exploration of several dominant factors pertinent to the perception and understanding of urban annihilation in the Syrian context.

Moreover, Damascus, Aleppo and Homs contain an impressive and diverse urban heritage highly valued by locals, more accurately termed 'living heritage'. Thus, the effective preservation of this cultural property requires the preservation of the cities themselves. Notably, significant changes have taken place in Syrian urban planning, some of which may appear chaotic while others have demonstrated respect for the value of urban heritage sites, exemplified by the case of Aleppo.

While experts focus primarily on damaged structures, it is imperative to recognise the profound emotional dimension of the loss of cities, resulting in feelings of pain and alienation across society. The Syrian collective memory has been deeply damaged, with the self-image of Syrians distorted by the extreme violence and dehumanisation of the past eight years. Efforts to rebuild Syrian cultural identity must now be more inclusive and diverse if the desired peacebuilding outcomes are to be achieved in the country.[8]

Finally, given that archaeological sites have featured prominently in the destruction, the term 'memorycide', referring to the erasure of public memory, is perhaps more fitting to describe what has transpired with the expansion of warfare beyond urban areas.[9]

---

7   Emma Cunliffe, Nibal Muhesen and Marina Lostal, 'The Destruction of Cultural Property in the Syrian Conflict: Legal Implications and Obligations', *International Journal of Cultural Property*, 23 (2016), 1–31.

8   Nibal Muhesen, 'Reconstructing Syrian Cultural Heritage: Mapping Challenges and Impacts Challenges, Strategies and High-Tech Application for Saving Cultural Heritage of Syria', *Oriental and European Archaeology Series* (2020/2021), 21–39.

9   Marina Lostal and Emma Cunliffe, 'Cultural Heritage that Heals: Factoring in Cultural Heritage Discourses in the Syrian Peace Building Process', *The Historic Environment: Policy & Practice*, 7 (2020), 1–13.

Post-conflict Urban Heritage and Reconstruction Plans

The reconstruction phase in Syria, literally *i'ādat al i'mār* (rebuilding), will face severe challenges as well as entail national and international responsibilities for those involved in the conflict. There is an urgent need to prepare optimal methods and strategies to rehouse affected communities, adapted to local needs able to be implemented on the ground immediately. This is the case in Aleppo, a city that embodies a dramatic dimension of the Syrian war.

It is clear that failure in post-war reconstruction strategies or inefficient rehabilitation programs may lead to the resumption of hostilities or revive tensions among Syrian groups. Several obstacles to rebuilding damaged Syrian cities will be encountered during the recovery phase, which are briefly enumerated as follows:

1. With the deliberate allocation of funds, the economic viability of current governmental institutions is likely to deteriorate, potentially rendering them virtually dysfunctional in the future.

2. Inefficient rebuilding polices could impede the return of displaced persons or refugees both inside and outside the country.

3. It is important to consider new demographic realities, such as the near doubling of populations due to refugees in cities like Damascus and Latakia.

4. Rebuilding efforts must include housing shattered communities, with hopes that the reconstruction of the old towns in Aleppo and Homs will pave the way for the return of refugees and displaced residents.

5. Comprehensive damage assessment is necessary, as a considerable number of lesser-known urban areas were destroyed during the war, indicating the extent of damage is likely higher than expected.

6. Syria is and will continue to be a hub for intensive rebuilding activities with the potential to attract local and foreign companies. However, these companies may view Syria's destroyed urban landscape predominately if not exclusively in terms of economic interest, showing little consideration for the fragility of local communities and their cultural heritage. Thus, caution should be exercised to ensure that public consultation is made a priority.

Ultimately, rebuilding will be a monumental task, and regional experiences have shown that the most destructive period for cultural heritage often comes in the aftermath of conflict, as seen in Beirut after the Civil War in Lebanon.[10]

Observations on Reconstruction Cases from Aleppo and Homs

Going forward, a number of principles should be respected in the rebuilding of Syrian cities. First and foremost, these efforts must engage the remaining local population and respect their traditional building practices. Drawing from past experiences like the aftermath of war in the Balkans, experts maintain that the rebuilding of cultural heritage sites encourages the return of displaced communities to their homelands.[11] Thus, the reconstruction of the old districts in Aleppo and Damascus can be expected to encourage the return and resettlement of displaced civilians, necessitating that their needs be considered in determining reconstruction priorities. Secondly, reconstruction efforts must seek to ensure that new demographic groups will be able to engage positively with their surroundings and reconnect with elements of their distinctive heritage.

Old Aleppo

The destruction inflicted upon the millennia-old urban and cultural heritage of the Ancient City of Aleppo is tragic. Prior to the conflict, the Ancient City was designated a UNESCO World Heritage Site, prompting Syrian archaeological authorities to document its buildings and introduce measures prohibiting the demolition or alteration of architectural features without proper authorisation. Of all localities in Syria, Aleppo was most severely affected by the wartime destruction of cultural heritage. Just to name the most important losses: the twelfth-century Citadel of Aleppo, the fourteenth-century traditional *souqs*

---

10 Assad Seif, 'Conceiving the Past: Fluctuations in a Multi-value System', *Conservation and Management of Archaeological Sites*, 11.3–4 (2009), 282–95.

11 Dacia Viejo-Rose, 'Reconstructing Heritage in the Aftermath of Civil War: Revisioning the Nation and the Implications of International Involvement', *Journal of Intervention and State Building: Special Issue on Cultural Interventions*, 7.2 (2013), 125–42.

[street markets] of the city, as well as the eighth-century Great Umayyad Mosque with its unique library and ornamented minaret.[12]

According to experts, the damage to historic buildings and archaeological sites is irreparable[13] (Figures 2.2 and 2.3).

Fig. 2.2 Urban destruction in Aleppo. Author's photograph, 2023, CC BY-NC-ND.

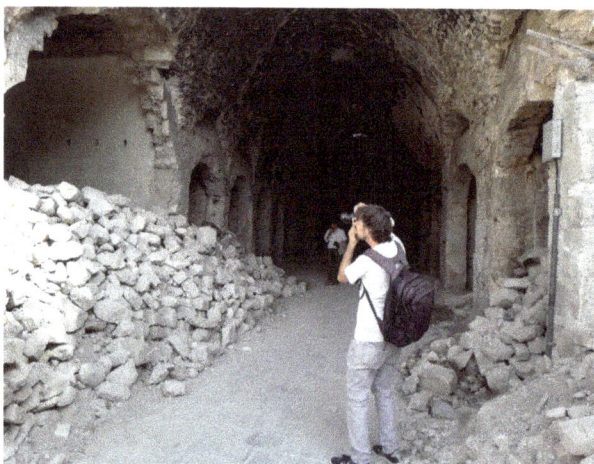

Fig. 2.3 Destruction, collapsing structures and rubble in the traditional bazar, which was the heart of the Ancient City of Aleppo. Author's photograph, 2023, CC BY-NC-ND.

---

12   DGAM, Report on the State of Conservation.
13   Mamoun Abdulkarim, *Syrian Archaeological Heritage 2016 Five Years of Crisis 2011–2015* (Damascus: The Directorate General of Antiquities and Museums, 2016).

Reconstruction efforts in Aleppo should start with the careful removal of rubble and clearing of the remnants of war. After this has been achieved, the excavation of the old city may be possible but should be undertaken in a focused and site-targeted manner without impeding rebuilding activities. Moreover, the authorities must provide secure storage facilities for archaeological artefacts in order to prevent any damage or loss.

Throughout these efforts, continuity should be maintained between the new city and Old Aleppo, ensuring the preservation of the traditional urban character in accordance with the collective memory of its inhabitants. Specific attention should be directed towards the preservation of traditional ways of life and crafts, which are an integral part of the city's intangible heritage. Additionally, any rehabilitation plans in Aleppo must comply with its status as a UNESCO World Heritage Site, rendering it subject to restrictions at both the national and international levels.[14] Finally, the imperative of community-driven reconstruction, responsive to local needs, merits re-emphasis.

Currently, the reconstruction of the Ancient City of Aleppo constitutes a joint effort between DGAM, UNESCO and the Aga Khan Foundation for Cultural Services. Syrian officials have entrusted the Agha Khan Foundation with the major restoration and preservation activities, particularly in the city's iconic old market, *souqs* and religious sites, which have sustained significant damage. According to the authorities, the initiative will be undertaken in full accordance with the principles, standards and conventions of international restoration at levels of implementation.[15]

Old Homs

Wide sections of the ancient town of Homs, as well as several surrounding urban districts, have been severely damaged by the Syrian war, with some areas entirely obliterated.

---

14 United Nations Educational, Scientific and Cultural Organization, 'Emergency Safeguarding of the Syrian Cultural Heritage', *UNESCO*, https://ich.unesco.org/en/projects/emergency-safeguarding-of-the-syrian-cultural-heritage-00386

15 Angus McDowall, 'Syria's Lost Heritage Stands Out in Aleppo's Broken Minarets' (1 May 2019), *Reuters*, https://www.reuters.com/article/uk-syria-security-heritage-idUKKCN1S7426

The reconstruction of Homs began after Syrian authorities established control over Old Homs. Officials have already planned and launched rebuilding projects in the destroyed district, including the restoration of the iconic Al-Zahrawi Palace, characterised by its beautiful architectural style dating back to the Ottoman period. Other notable initiatives include the large-scale restoration of the Khalid Ibn al-Walid Mosque as well as the Old Market in Homs, significant landmarks of the city.[16]

Reconstruction of Destroyed Sites or Shattered Communities?

We will turn our attention now to two topics: firstly, how locals perceive the importance of heritage reconstruction to the resumption of daily life, and secondly, the particularities of the Syrian context. There are divergent views on the issue of rebuilding destroyed heritage sites in contexts of devastated urban infrastructure, including facilities such as schools and residential areas. This is the case in the city of Aleppo, where researchers observe a lack of consensus among locals on whether or not rebuilding heritage sites should be seen as a top priority.[17]

Further, it is important to note that reconstruction policies in the post-Civil War period in Beirut showed that at least parts of the destroyed town should be kept as a reminder of the atrocities of the war.[18] In the Syrian context, such a decision is difficult because, on the one hand, preserving remains of the destroyed town or building might constantly trigger the memory of war-associated hostilities, but on the other, it would serve to send a message to the children to at least not repeat the mistakes committed by their parents and encourage them to engage in the national politics of reconciliation. It can also be assumed that preserving some parts of the memory of the war in Syria would provide some comfort to the community by continuously underlining the importance of avoiding armed conflicts and mutual hostilities, as was seen in the Yellow House of Beirut. This house is an outstanding

---

16   Abdulkarim, *Syrian Archaeological Heritage 2016*.
17   Benjamin Iskhan and Lynn Meksell, 'Heritage Protection and Reconstruction in Syria after the Islamic State', in *The Palgrave Encyclopedia of Cultural Heritage and Conflict*, ed. by I. Saloul and B. Baillie (London: Palgrave Macmillan, 2020), n.p.
18   Sandes, 'Urban Cultural Heritage and Armed Conflict', pp. 309–11.

historic (Ottoman) structure that was majorly damaged in the Civil War and then condemned to demolition in 1997. However, after renovation, and following great efforts by Lebanese heritage experts, it was decided that the house should become a war museum as well as, more recently, a site for many artistic and cultural activities.[19] However, a significant difference from the Lebanese experience is visible in the fact that Aleppo, the most affected Syrian city, holds the status of a UNESCO World Heritage Site, which imposes significant restrictions with respect to the rebuilding of the ancient city.

Before summing up, it is important to touch upon the question of reconstruction of destroyed places and how, if these places are to be restored, such a process could be carried out. The following questions emerge concerning the reconstruction of heritage sites and monuments:

- Should these sites and monuments be rebuilt exactly as they were before sustaining damage in the spirit of continuity, or should they be updated and modernised in the spirit of innovation?

- Does the restoration effort attest to the cultural existence of past groups?

- What role do memorialisation and remembrance play in the restoration project, in the context of the country's post-conflict rehabilitation?

As these questions indicate, the form and nature of reconstructed architecture is likely to have a significant impact on the success of social and cultural interaction among communities in post-war Syria.[20] Moreover, the reconstruction of damaged sites and monuments will inevitably pose the challenge of maintaining the authenticity of these sites while utilising cutting-edge documentation and protection techniques. This requires prioritising cultural continuity in order to secure the vestiges of the past while remaining open to progressive approaches.

---

19 Seif , 'Conceiving the Past', Fluctuations in a Multi Value System'.
20 Dacia Viejo-Rose and Marie Louise Stig Sørensen, 'Cultural Heritage and Armed Conflict: New Questions for an Old Relationship', in *The Palgrave Handbook of Contemporary Heritage Research*, ed. by Edmund Waterton and Steve Watson (London: Palgrave Macmillan, 2015), pp. 281–96.

In confronting the issue of reconstructing Syrian urban heritage, this research advocates consideration of three main perspectives. The first of these is the Western approach, which privileges a 'return to the pre-conflict status', with restored sites fully resembling their pre-war iteration. In Syria, this task is difficult but not impossible, as substantial amounts of data, including detailed maps and photographic archives, exist pertaining to the country's destroyed heritage sites. This includes domestic resources like the DGAM archives as well as foreign materials, such as the archives of international archaeological missions. However, this paradigm is undermined by the fact that the pre-conflict state of most destroyed Syrian heritage sites, such as Palmyra, reflects the extensive restoration efforts undertaken in the 1960s and 1970s. Furthermore, the use of modern restoration techniques, including three- and four-dimensional technology, raises the question of whether the outcomes of such restoration can truly reflect the authenticity of these sites. Indeed, modern or historically inaccurate structural modifications during the restoration project could diminish the sites' historical value, underscoring the imperative of utilising the right tools and personnel in the renovation process.

The second perspective is a locally based concept, emphasising the use of traditional building materials and construction techniques as well as local expertise. Although the final outcome of this approach may not differ significantly from the previous one, it entails greater levels of local participation in restoration and engagement in decision-making, enabling residents to voice concerns and resulting in a tailored project and use of funds that meets local needs. However, this approach may carry a greater risk of failure, potentially leading to clashes between state and local reconstruction priorities or irreparable damage during restoration efforts.

The third and final perspective is based on collective memory, calling to mind the concept of *ansanat al-mākān*, or 'humanisation of place', through the prioritisation of memorialisation and remembrance. This approach entails preserving the destruction and vandalism inflicted on heritage sites as a publicly visible reminder of not only the barbarity and wanton destruction of conflict but the unique history of the sites themselves. This is particularly important as these sites are more than simply stones and rubble—they embody an essential part of the local character, and their destruction has become integral to the story of the place and its people.[21] Limited-scale restoration projects of this kind must necessarily focus on the most significant features of these sites and those of greatest local interest. However, this approach will almost certainly conflict with state intentions to regenerate life in these places by resuming tourism activities.

Conclusion

With its diversity and richness, Syrian urban heritage represents a sensitive intersection between the past embodied in the remains of heritage sites and the present reflected in the daily lives of its inhabitants. It is necessary to strike a delicate balance between meeting the population's housing needs and preserving the urban heritage of Syria's cities and historic districts. These structures, including mosques and traditional houses, were already fragile before the war and have suffered significant damage during the conflict.

While the physical dimension of reconstruction efforts is impressive, the psychological aspect of rebuilding is even more critical to the survival of affected communities. Reconnecting the population with their new cities is certain to pose a major challenge for future reconstruction policies. The destruction of urban heritage in cities like Aleppo and Homs significantly impacted the local cultural identity of these communities.

The best path forward in the reconstruction of Syrian cities would secure the future without obliterating the memory of the past or distorting local cultural and social identities. Only time will tell if this is possible, considering that it hinges upon both national and international commitment to the rebuilding process, as well as external factors and new threats.[22]

---

21   Ibid.
22   Notably, in February of 2023, a devastating earthquake struck large parts of Syria and Turkey, leading to full-fledged regional disaster. Thousands of people were killed and tens of thousands displaced amid massive urban destruction. This tragic event underscores the imperative to raise concerns about the survival of historic buildings and archaeological sites, particularly given the significant damage sustained by heritage sites already under restoration, such as Aleppo's Omayyad Mosque. For more on this, see DGAM and UNESCO,

The survival of Syrian urban heritage will entail a complex preservation process, given the dual threats of human destruction and unpredictable natural disasters. Accompanied by political stability and economic growth, common usage and a shared understanding of heritage can pave the way for reconciliation among divergent Syrian factions. Heritage can thus play a critical role in fostering social stability and societal healing by uniting Syrians around common values and shared history.

Bibliography

Abdulkarim, Mamoun, *Syrian Archaeological Heritage 2016 Five Years of Crisis 2011–2015* (Damascus: The Directorate General of Antiquities and Museums, 2016).

Bartels, Rogier, 'The Classification of Armed Conflicts by International Criminal Courts and Tribunals', *International Criminal Law Review*, 20 (2020), 595–668.

Coward, Martin, *Urbicide: The Politics of Urban Destruction* (New York: Routledge, 2009), pp. 186–89.

Cunliffe, Emma, Muhesen, Nibal and Lostal, Marina, 'The Destruction of Cultural Property in the Syrian Conflict: Legal Implications and Obligations', *International Journal of Cultural Property*, 23 (2016), 1–31.

Directorate General of Antiquities and Museums (DGAM), *Report on the State of Conservation of Syrian Cultural Heritage Sites* (Damascus: DGAM, 2021).

Directorate General of Antiquities and Museums (DGAM) and UNESCO, *Joint Damages Report on Survey Conducted on 25/27th Feb 2023* (n.p.: DGAM and UNESCO, 2023).

Gelin, Mathilde, *L'Archéologie en Syrie et au Liban à l'Epoque du Mandat 1919–1946* (Paris: Librairie Orientaliste, 2002).

Iskhan, Benjamin and Meksell, Lynn, 'Heritage Protection and Reconstruction in Syria after the Islamic State', in *The Palgrave Encyclopedia of Cultural Heritage and Conflict*, ed. by I. Saloul and B. Baillie (London: Palgrave Macmillan, 2020), n.p.

Joint Damages Report on Survey Conducted on 25/27th Feb 2023 (n.p.: DGAM and UNESCO, 2023); UNESCO, 'Earthquake in Syria and Türkiye: UNESCO Offers Support' (7 February 2023), *UNESCO*, https://www.unesco.org/en/articles/earthquake-syria-and-turkiye-unesco-offers-support

Lostal, Marina and Cunliffe, Emma, 'Cultural Heritage that Heals: Factoring in Cultural Heritage Discourses in the Syrian Peace Building Process', *The Historic Environment: Policy & Practice*, 7 (2020), 1–13.

McDowall, Angus, 'Syria's Lost Heritage Stands Out in Aleppo's Broken Minarets' (1 May 2019), *Reuters*, https://www.reuters.com/article/uk-syria-security-heritage-idUKKCN1S7426

Muhesen, Nibal, 'Reconstructing Syrian Cultural Heritage: Mapping Challenges and Impacts Challenges, Strategies and High-Tech Application for Saving Cultural Heritage of Syria', *Oriental and European Archaeology Series* (2020/2021), 21–39

Sabrine, Isber, Alyhia, Abdulhman and Barkat, Mahmoud, *The Impact of the 2023-Earthquake on Archaeological Locations in Northwest Syria* (n.p.: Heritage for Peace, 2023), https://ansch.heritageforpeace.org/wp-content/uploads/2023/03/the-impact-of-the-2023-earthquake-on-the-archaeological-locations-on-the-Syrian-coast.pdf

Sandes, Catherine, 'Urban Cultural Heritage and Armed Conflict: The Case of Beirut Central District', in *Cultural Heritage in the Crosshairs: Protecting Cultural Property during Conflict*, ed. by Joris Kila and James Zeidler (Leiden: Brill, 2013), pp. 287–315

Seif, Assad, 'Conceiving the Past: Fluctuations in a Multi-value System', *Conservation and Management of Archaeological Sites*, 11.3–4 (2009), 282–95.

United Nations Educational, Scientific and Cultural Organization, 'Emergency Safeguarding of the Syrian Cultural Heritage', *UNESCO*, https://ich.unesco.org/en/projects/emergency-safeguarding-of-the-syrian-cultural-heritage-00386

United Nations Educational, Scientific and Cultural Organization, 'Earthquake in Syria and Türkiye: UNESCO Offers Support' (7 February 2023), *UNESCO*, https://www.unesco.org/en/articles/earthquake-syria-and-turkiye-unesco-offers-support

Viejo-Rose, Dacia, 'Reconstructing Heritage in the Aftermath of Civil War: Revisioning the Nation and the Implications of International Involvement', *Journal of Intervention and State Building: Special Issue on Cultural Interventions*, 7.2 (2013), 125–42.

Viejo-Rose, Dacia and Sørensen, Marie Louise Stig, 'Cultural Heritage and Armed Conflict: New Questions for an Old Relationship', in The Palgrave Handbook of Contemporary Heritage Research, ed. by Edmund Waterton and Steve Watson (London: Palgrave Macmillan, 2015), pp. 281–91.

II. MODERN CITIES AND RESIDENTIAL DESIGN IN MOROCCO

3. Housing and Local Identity through the Prism of Urban Planning Policy in Morocco

Soufiane Essebbar

Introduction

The fields of urban planning, architecture and housing are of paramount importance due to their significant impact on economic, environmental and social dimensions. In Morocco, policies governing these areas have incorporated a variety of legal and regulatory frameworks since the establishment of the French protectorate in 1912, making it difficult to monitor their provisions.

In this chapter, I analyse the salient factors shaping architectural and urban expression in Morocco from an urban planning perspective. This study aims to illuminate how urban planning policies in Morocco influence housing and local identity in the context of urbanisation. Through this research, I endeavour to understand the treatment of local identity throughout Morocco's development, examining various approaches such as the culturalist and progressive movements.

This investigation reveals that the adoption of French urban planning methods has generated a crisis of identity and cultural expression that has compromised the efficiency of Moroccan cities for more than a century. The trend towards universalist standardisation of space has preserved stereotypical urban forms that conflict with local architectural identity and are thus incapable of meeting the

    https://doi.org/10.11647/OBP.0460.03

contemporary population's diverse and evolving needs. The findings can assist policymakers in developing a system that corresponds to local socio-cultural and spatial specificities in order to counteract the trivialisation of the urban environment.

Accelerated urban growth has become a global reality. Faced with this phenomenon, regional planning specialists have turned to urban planning in order to manage and guide urban expansion in the short, medium and long terms. However, in the current international context, urban policies introduced through spatial planning are often flawed and unable to keep step with rapid changes in the configuration of urban space. This gap impedes effective coordination between public and private actions as well as the socio-economic development of cities.

Morocco is no exception to this constraining reality, illustrating the inability of the current urban planning system to provide a structured and coherent framework for sustainable urban development.

In this contribution, we highlight certain factors that have influenced architectural and urban expression in Morocco, including housing, from an urban planning perspective. An examination of existing literature and scientific research reveals that these diverse urban phenomena have attracted the attention of researchers from various fields, including spatial, political, social and economic studies. However, urban planning and architectural regulations have rarely provided a solid foundation for understanding urban phenomena and housing processes.

The methodology adopted in this study is rooted in both historical and empirical approaches. First, I use deductive methods based on preliminary theoretical and historical investigations on the subject of housing in Morocco. I then employed inductive reasoning based on empirical investigations of architectural regulations, drawing generalised conclusions regarding the impact of these determinants on Moroccan housing.

Housing in Morocco: Between Cultural Conservation and Western Acculturation

The French protectorate that governed Morocco between 1912 and 1956 viewed colonial cities as laboratories for architectural and urban planning experimentation.[1] In 1914, Resident-General Louis-Hubert Lyautey invited urban planners and legal specialists to Morocco with the aim of designing a development framework for new European cities and ensuring compliance with the necessary regulations for its implementation. He entrusted Guillaume de Tarde, the Director of Civil Affairs at the time, with drafting the legislation for colonial agglomerations,[2] while appointing Henri Prost to manage the architectural and town planning services of the protectorate.

Colonial architects were confronted with several issues in the making of the modern city, including the presence of traditional urban fabrics (medinas), cultural and religious differences and social segregation. Throughout the history of French colonisation in Morocco, two approaches were adopted to address these issues, which are examined in this section.

Culturalist Expression (Henri Prost)

Culturalist expression was a new architectural approach inspired by traditional Moroccan architecture. It resulted in a blend of Moroccan architectural style and certain European elements, giving rise to the Arabisance movement.[3]

The French colonial administration demonstrated a degree of appreciation for Moroccan Arab-Muslim architecture, with the Department of Fine Arts and Historical Monuments conducting exhaustive research on Moroccan medinas and monuments in an effort to preserve Moroccan architectural elements and principles.[4] However, this was also strategic, with the architectural fusion of Arabisance used as a tactic to ease the acculturation of Moroccans. The political manipulation of visual elements was intended to cultivate an alliance

---

1   Jean Pierre Gaudin, 'Tours et détours coloniaux de l'urbanisme français', *Dossiers des Séminaires Techniques, Territoires et Sociétés*, 4.4 (1988).

2   Guillaume de Tarde, 'L'urbanisme aux colonies et dans les pays tropicaux', in *L'urbanisme en Afrique du nord. Rapport général*, ed. by Jean Royer, 2 vols (Paris: Les éditions de l'urbanisme, 1932), I, 27–31.

3   Arabisance refers to the architectural style which flourished in the Maghreb region throughout the twentieth century, closely connected with French colonisation. This imitative style is subject to more liberal interpretations, combining European stylistic elements and Arab influences, akin to the 'neo-Moorish style'.

4   Gaudin, Tours et détours coloniaux de l'urbanisme français'.

between local authorities and the population, as demonstrated by François Béguin's 1983 book, entitled *Arabisances*.[5]

Fig. 3.1 Photograph of Bank Al-Maghrib on Avenue Dar al-Makhzen in Rabat (currently Avenue Mohammed V), featuring Arabisance-style facades. Photograph by Michael Ball (2021), Wikimedia, https://commons.wikimedia. org/wiki/File:Bank_Al-Maghrib,_Rabat.jpg#/media/File:Bank-Al-Maghrib,_ Rabat.jpg, CC0 1.0.

As a result, the reappropriation of traditional construction techniques developed differently across Morocco, Algeria and Tunisia, according to varying contextual factors such as state and committee encouragement or the private initiatives of individual architects. The unifying objective was to reify the authority of the French protectorate, following several years of neoclassicism being perceived by indigenous populations as the style of colonialism.

In 1914, Prost introduced the concept of 'surface architecture',[6] denoting the contrast between Westernised interiors and Orientalised

---

5   François Béguin, *Arabisances: Décor architectural et tracé urbain en Afrique du nord, 1830–1950* (Paris: Bordas Editions, 1993).

6   Abdelmajid Arrif, 'La ville coloniale au Maroc: objet de savoirs, objet de projets. Sciences sociales, Architecture, Urbanisme', paper delivered at the seminar 'Architectures exportées: transferts, expérimentations, métissages' (Laboratoire Urbama Université de Tours, équipe LAA Ecole d'Architecture de Paris-La Villette et Laboratoire Ladrhaus Ecole d'Architecture de Versailles, 1993).

exteriors. He proposed employing Western construction methods within buildings while decorating their exterior facades in the Arabisance style. Thus, facades were adorned with decorative elements inspired by Moroccan architecture, using local materials such as *zellij* [azulejos in French, azulejo tiles in English], carved wood, plaster and tile, as well as incorporating Moroccan architectural elements like domes, arcades, columns and ornate friezes.

However, the separation of 'native' and European quarters was an important principle in the design of colonial cities, intended to ensure the preservation and protection of the medina. Paradoxically, the desire to protect the medinas also contributed to their gradual deterioration.

Moreover, Lyautey's theory of separation precipitated a change in the perception and treatment of Muslim cities. While the layout and construction of the colonial city embodied a commitment to rational principles and modern methods, the Muslim city was perceived through the lens of an imposed status as an object of picturesque aestheticism, condemning it to stagnation.[7] Consequently, medinas were integrated into new developments and spatially annexed as homogeneous zones, suffocating them from the outside. Excessive constraints consigned these areas to inertia, and restricted them from their natural process of expansion and development, leaving them to slowly decay over time. This transformation rendered the medinas as artefacts to be appreciated from a distance in the modern colonial city, but left them unable to grow and adapt alongside their surroundings.

Progressive Expression (Michel Ecochard)

The end of the 1940s was marked by significant migration to the new colonial towns. Michel Ecochard, the architect responsible for the new development plans, introduced new forms that departed from the Arabisance movement and colonial culturalist expression in favour of the principles of modern architecture. In adopting a progressive and

---

7   Said Mouline, 'Architecture Métissée et Patrimoine', in *Old Cultures in New Worlds, 8th ICOMOS General Assembly and International Symposium Programme Report— Compte rendu* (Washington, DC: US/ICOMOS, 1987), pp. 715–22.

standardised approach, the goal was to accommodate a maximum number of Moroccan households through the creation of low-cost housing according to the so-called 'Ecochard grid'.[8] In this context, Jean Dethier has argued that a theoretical uniformity is supposed to reduce the multiple variants of society, geography and manners, ethnic groups, climate and materials to a single common denominator; this is the schematic image of a typical Moroccan.[9]

In the 1950s, the Carrières Centrales District became the first effective application of the Ecochard grid. The district comprised a horizontal and vertical concentration, demonstrating the flexibility of the district's fabric and incorporating various construction types. The main objective of the project was to provide Moroccans with diverse patio houses in order to temporarily eliminate slums with modern high-rise buildings featuring openings and superimposed patios.

At the district level, Ecochard devised an urban model structured around neighbourhood units,[10] comprising dwellings, pedestrian paths and local amenities such as mosques, traditional bakeries, *hammams* [bathhouses] and *madrasas* [schools]. This model aligns with Clarence Perry's concept of 'neighbourhood units',[11] which Ecochard encountered during a 1945 study trip to the United States with Le Corbusier and Vladimir Bodiansky.

In 1951, George Candilis joined ATBAT-Afrique, a subsidiary of the Atelier des Bâtisseurs,[12] of which he became director. Ecochard tasked Candilis with implementing a project in Carrières Centrales and proposed an alternative to the horizontal grid. Candilis' main contribution was

---

8   These popular housing districts included lots measuring 64 square metres for the construction of houses intended for the lower classes.

9   Author's translation, for original quote see Jean Dethier, 'Soixante ans d'urbanisme au Maroc. L'évolution des idées et des réalisations', *Bulletin Economique et Social du Maroc*, 118–19 (1970), 5–56 (p. 35).

10   The concept of the neighbourhood unit was developed during the 1930s in the United States to refer to a group of dwellings formed around an elementary school, which constitutes the basic unit of development in North American suburbs.

11   Perry Clarence, *The Neighborhood Unit: A Scheme of Arrangement for the Family Life Community*, Regional Plan of New York, 7 vols (New York: Regional Plan Association, 1929), I.

12   Atelier des Bâtisseurs [The Workshop of Builders] was founded in 1945 by engineer Vladimir Bodiansky, Le Corbusier, André Wogenscky and Jacques-Louis Lefebvre as a research centre where architects, engineers and technicians work in a multidisciplinary manner. Bodiansky ensured the technical direction.

his idea of 'the habitat of the greatest number', inspired by Ecochard himself, with whom Shadrach Woods and Candilis presented their work in Morocco in 1953 during the Ninth International Congress of Modern Architecture (CIAM).

The collaboration between architects Georges Candilis, Shadrach Woods, and engineers Henri Piot and Vladimir Bodiansky through ATBAT-Afrique resulted in three typological and radical collective buildings arranged in a 'U' formation in the centre of Ecochard's horizontal grid. These collective buildings, known as the Semiramis[13] and the Nid d'abeilles[14], represented the French protectorate's first effort to build new housing for the colonised rather than the colonisers. However, while the intention was to provide workers and rural migrants with affordable housing options, the newly developed model proved too expensive for most slum dwellers.[15]

Moreover, the concept of building climate control was introduced through the use of buffer spaces between interiors and exteriors. Passageways, stairs, balconies, covered patios and loggias created an interplay of solid masses (buildings and structures) and the open spaces (voids) around them, accentuated by daylight. The cusps were inspired by the architecture of the High Atlas Mountains and served a particular function: projecting components defined the boundaries of public space, while recessed elements delineated the thresholds of private space. The focal point of the ATBAT-Afrique team's approach was intermediate spaces and their integration into the production of high-density housing.

---

13   The Semiramis, oriented along an east-west axis, integrates the sloping terrain into its architectural design. Accommodations are arranged on alternating floors, accessible by front passageways leading to private patios. Apartments provide approximately 35 square metres of living space with simple furnishings. An external staircase connects the passageways to the patio, vestibule, kitchen area, wet rooms and two bedrooms. At least three elements mark the transition from public to private space: staircase-landings, galleries and patios.

14   The Nid d'abeilles [honeycomb] building is oriented along a north-south axis, with passageways on the north side. Due to the closure of the suspended patios, it is no longer recognisable today.

15   Michel Ecochard, *Casablanca: Le roman d'une ville* (Paris: Editions de Paris, 1955), p. 103.

Fig. 3.2 The Nid d'abeilles building upon completion in 1954. Photograph by *L'Architecture d'Aujourd'hui* (1954), Wikimedia, https://commons.wikimedia.org/ wiki/File:L%27Architecture_d%27Aujourd%27hui_December_1954.jpg#/media/ File:L'Architecture_d'Aujourd'hui_December_1954.jpg, public domain.

Although both Prost's and Ecochard's conceptions acknowledged the cultural gap between European and Muslim populations, an essential difference emerged in their approaches to the urban development of the Moroccan city: while the former sought to preserve native architectural characteristics, the latter anticipated their gradual disappearance. For Ecochard, this disappearance would result from 'the rise of the standard of living',[16] viewed as a process of acculturation to the 'modern'—that is, Western—way of life.

Despite this significant difference, the idea of Moroccan specificity in housing has held a prominent place in the technical culture of urban planning services. The influence of this dimension continued after the country's independence in 1956, evident in the 1964 decree on economic housing subdivisions. This distinguishes Moroccan town planning culture from other Maghreb countries, reflecting the recognition among architects and urban planners of the vibrant tradition in local culture. Ecochard himself noted this, although he appears to have interpreted the closing of external openings not as an expression of cultural resistance but rather as a sign of backwardness with regard to modern urban hygiene standards.

In this context, it is apparent that Morocco inherited an urban planning service reformed at the doctrinal level by Ecochard's architectural and urban planning influence, which saw his notion of economic housing incorporated into the administration services. The urban planning doctrine established by Ecochard did not undergo any significant changes after Moroccan independence. He left behind a well-trained team in his urban planning principles, and his legacy included several key elements: decentralisation options, an active economic housing policy, considerable land reserves, updated and completed legislation, new concepts of town planning, and an impressive series of general and detailed plans for numerous agglomerations, particularly Casablanca. These contributions ensured that Ecochard's influence on Moroccan urban planning remained significant and enduring long after independence.[17] This legacy of doctrine and experimentation later served as a reference for the 1964 economic subdivision plan (Decree Number 26 XII 1964).

The Economic Housing Subdivision: A Hybrid Urban Form

According to the High Commission for Planning, the distribution of households by housing type in urban areas showed a notable increase in modern Moroccan houses and apartments between 2004 and 2014, with

---

16   Ibid., p. 103.
17   Jean Dethier, 'Soixante ans d'urbanisme au Maroc', p. 35.

the former rising from 62.6% to 65% and the latter from 12.4% to 17.5%. Meanwhile the share of traditional houses declined during this period from 8.1% to 5.5%, as did the occupancy of basic housing or slums, which decreased from 8.2% to 5.2%. In rural areas, although rural-type housing remained dominant at 64.1%, a significant increase in modern Moroccan houses was recorded from 13.6% in 2004 to 25.9% in 2014.

Table 3.1 Distribution of households (%) by type of dwelling and place of residence in 2004 and 2014 (Source: Haut-Commissariat au Plan du Maroc 2014).

Type of dwelling	According to the census of 2004 (RGPH* 2004)			According to the census of 2014 (RGPH 2014)		
	Urban	Rural	Total	Urban	Rural	Total
Villa/villa floor	3.3	0.3	2.2	4.5	0.8	3.2
Apartment	12.4	0.1	7.6	17.5	0.3	11.6
Traditional Moroccan house	8.1	4.8	6.8	5.5	4.8	5.2
Modern Moroccan house	62.6	13.6	43.4	65.0	25.9	51.6
Room in an establishment	0.3	0.2	0.3	0.2	0.2	0.2
Slum	8.2	5.7	7.2	5.2	3.1	4.5
Non-residential room used for housing	0.8	0.5	0.7	0.4	0.2	0.3
Rural house	1.1	72.8	29.1	1.3	64.0	22.8
Other	1.5	1.0	1.3	0.5	0.6	0.6
Not Declared	1.6	1.0	1.3	-	0.1	0.0
Total	100.0	100.0	100.0	100.0	100.0	100.0
Number of dwellings	3,435,134	2,207,055	5,642,189	4,806,322	2,505,634	7,311,956

* Recensement Général de la Population et de l'Habitat = RGPH [General Census of the Population and Housing].

The modern Moroccan house[18] has been selected for the focus of this study as, according to the 2014 general population and housing census, it constitutes the most representative form of housing in Morocco.

---

18 'Modern Moroccan house' is the official term used by the competent authorities and architectural services, including the High Commission for Planning, from which our data is sourced. The diverse Western terminology used to denote various types of residential units does not seem to have a direct equivalent in

The Moroccan Modern House in Urban Planning Documents: A Hybrid Urban Form

The economic housing subdivision is part of the lineage of Ecochard's sanitary framework and the Moroccan housing tradition that it was meant to revive. The articles of the 1964 decree regulate the urban form of economic housing development, permitting small plots of 60 to 100 square metres, with three adjoining boundaries, provided there is a courtyard. The surface area cannot exceed 16 square metres for a single-storey building and 20 square metres for a two-storey building.

However, it is worth noting that the 1964 decree deviates from Ecochard's urban planning principles in two respects. First, it legitimises a derogation from the horizontality recommended by Ecochard, which discouraged densification by adding additional floors to Moroccan dwellings, favouring verticality with more space between buildings. Second, the decree appears to make a concession to those advocating for the production of 'new medinas', which Ecochard opposed. Thus, in a way, the decree undermines the development of vertical buildings as envisioned by Ecochard, legitimising the 'new medinas' (neo-traditional housing)[19] while establishing minimum regulations to ensure the sanitation of buildings. Nevertheless, this economic housing development formula has been promoted by both public and private initiatives and has proven highly successful in peripheral extensions. It enables the progressive commitment of the lot purchaser to their construction efforts.

In the years following the 1964 decree, the modern Moroccan house model spread throughout the country without any consideration for regional specificities and local identity. Particular emphasis was placed on hygiene measures, concrete construction procedures, sunlight exposure and ventilation. As an example, we consider two modern Moroccan houses, one in the south (Figure 3.3) and one in the north (Figure 3.4). Despite vast regional differences in culture, lifestyles, habits, climate

---

Arabic, particularly when referring to the specific forms of apartments and houses that make up the current typology of urban housing in Morocco. The term currently used for buildings in economic housing subdivisions is *dar*, which translates to 'house'. This bears a certain resemblance to the generic term used for urban housing in nineteenth-century France.

19   André Adam, *Casablanca, essai sur la transformation de la société marocaine au contact de l'Occident* (Paris: CNRS, 1968).

and traditional construction materials and colour palettes, these houses appear remarkably similar, suggesting a shared cultural context. In reality, however, this similarity stems from the standardisation of architecture and the prevalence of 'typical plans' in urban planning documents.

By making certain concessions to traditional typology such as courtyards, courtyard-facing fenestration and accessible terraces, the architectural models generated by the 1964 decree and occasional standardised plans enforced in state subdivisions over the last four decades introduced organisational forms borrowed from Western conceptualisations of housing at the urban and domestic levels. The layout mirrors that of conventional Western apartments, with the typical assortment of rooms arranged according to the typical partition between daytime and nighttime areas. This composition diverges significantly from the traditional Moroccan house structure, which distinguishes between *Bīt al-ḍiyāf* [guest room], *Buyūt al-galās* and *Buyūt al-naᶜās* [living rooms and sleeping rooms]. Furthermore, the standardised plan essentially relegates the interior courtyard to a lighting function, greatly diminishing its traditional symbolic and functional role in the Moroccan house. Thus, inhabitants are forced to overlook this imposed Western structure in order to reinscribe elements in accordance with their way of life.

Fig. 3.3 A modern Moroccan house in the southern city of Laayoune. Author's photograph, 2020, CC BY-NC-ND.

Fig. 3.4 A modern Moroccan house in the northern city of Tetouan. Author's photograph, 2020, CC BY-NC-ND.

Interior Redistribution of the Moroccan Modern House: The Necessity of a Central Space

Moroccan homeowners have demonstrated the ability to achieve a sense of spaciousness by maximising the internal distribution of their homes on small plots, utilising knowledge of the traditional house. However, this effect can only be fully realised by transforming the house into a truly centralised interior space. Subdivision houses, which partially face the street, rarely present a focus towards a central point such as the patio of the traditional house. The courtyard, mandated by law, is situated in a corner of the plot and does not occupy more than the position that allows it to serve as the centre. Nevertheless, inhabitants manage to regain this sense of centrality by redefining the internal partitioning of the home.

In summary, in order to adapt the hybrid model of the subdivision house to align with homeowners' mental image of the perfect urban dwelling for their family, the landowner in an economic subdivision must implement certain decisions and interventions concerning the selection of the plot, its orientation towards the street and its interior redistribution. This will require making alterations across various levels of the house and reorganising spaces to capitalise on the flexibility of the posts/slabs construction system. These modifications will enable these structures to accommodate the needs and expectations that govern family life in the city.

Intimacy within Domestic Space: Bipartition between the Family Space and the Guest Space

The standard architectural plans provided by the administration in 1964 organise residential buildings as stacks of single-family apartments comprising a living room, kitchen, bathrooms, and two bedrooms. A common layout orients the living room and one bedroom towards the street while the other bedroom and the kitchen open onto the legally mandated interior courtyard. From the perspective of the architect or urban planner, the two or three identical levels arranged in this way are designed to accommodate small families with no necessary relation to one another.

It is important to highlight the difficulties posed by this situation. The courtyard, which serves as the central point of space distribution in a traditional Moroccan house, is now intended for the family residing on the ground floor. Furthermore, the privacy of the ground floor is compromised by the overlooking views from the apartments on the upper floors. This arrangement is incompatible with the norms for protecting family privacy.[20] Thus, the modern interpretation of tradition that the architect or urban planner claims to offer becomes obsolete, with the courtyard used to discard various items unwanted by the ground-floor family and as a light source for the entire building. Similar observations could be made regarding the use of the terrace.

Some families undertake extensive reorganisation of their living spaces to harmonise their arrangements with traditional values, despite the challenges posed by moving partitions. Consequently, families often incorporate the patio into their house, transforming it into part of their living space to ensure their privacy. This practice directly contradicts the original design intentions of the architect.

---

20   Jean-Charles Depaule and Jean-Luc Arnaud, *A travers le mur* (Paris: Editions Parenthèses, 1985).

Moreover, a common theme in these redistributions is clearly distinguishing the *Bīt al-ḍiyāf* from the *Buyūt al-galās* and *Buyūt al-naʿās*. A *Marāḥ* [vestibule] is often introduced, making it possible to delineate one of these two spaces and correct previous design flaws that required women to cross a visible part of the living room to access the kitchen, the toilet, or to exit the house.[21] In traditional Moroccan households, such visibility was often problematic due to cultural norms surrounding gendered privacy and the expectation that women remain out of sight from male guests.

Conclusion

In examining the intricate interplay between urban planning policies and housing in Morocco, this chapter has highlighted the profound impact of colonial legacies and contemporary planning doctrines on the architectural and urban landscape. Our analysis has underscored the tension between cultural preservation and Western acculturation, revealing how French colonial urban planning methods have created a crisis of identity and cultural expression in Moroccan cities.

The legacy of Henri Prost's culturalist approach and Michel Ecochard's progressive expression continues to shape Moroccan urban planning. Prost's efforts to blend Moroccan and European architectural styles through the Arabisance movement aimed to ease the acculturation of Moroccans while preserving traditional aesthetics. In contrast, Ecochard's introduction of modern architectural principles and the Ecochard grid sought to accommodate rapid urbanisation and provide low-cost housing, albeit often at the expense of local architectural identity.

The post-independence period saw the introduction of the 1964 economic subdivision plan, which, while rooted in Ecochard's sanitary framework, deviated from his principles in key areas. This plan facilitated the proliferation of modern Moroccan houses, often characterised by standardised architectural forms that overlooked regional specificities

---

21   Daniel Pinson and Mohamed Zakrani, 'L'adaptation d'un système d'habitat composite: le lotissement économique au Maroc', in *Stratégies urbaines dans les pays en voie de développement: politiques et pratiques sociales en matière d'urbanisme et d'habitat*, ed. by N. Haumont and M. Alain (Paris: L'Harmattan, 1987), pp. 313–27.

and local identities. The economic housing development model promoted both public and private initiatives, resulting in widespread adoption across Morocco. However, the standardisation of architecture and the prevalence of 'typical plans' have led to a homogenisation of urban forms, diminishing the traditional symbolic and functional roles of elements such as courtyards. Homeowners, in their efforts to align their living arrangements with traditional values, have undertaken extensive reorganisation of spaces, often incorporating patios into their houses to ensure privacy. This practice contradicts the original design intentions of architects and highlights the ongoing struggle to reconcile modern urban planning with cultural heritage.

Ultimately, our study reveals the necessity of developing urban planning policies that are sensitive to local socio-cultural and spatial specificities. By recognising and integrating the diverse needs of contemporary populations, policymakers can counteract the trivialisation of the urban environment and foster sustainable development that respects and preserves Morocco's rich architectural heritage. The challenges posed by accelerated urban growth and the shortcomings of existing urban policies underscore the urgency of this task, as Morocco continues to navigate the complexities of modernisation and cultural identity.

Bibliography

Adam, André, *Casablanca, essai sur la transformation de la société marocaine au contact de l'Occident* (Paris: CNRS, 1968).

Arrif, Abdelmajid, 'La ville coloniale au Maroc: objet de savoirs, objet de projets. Sciences sociales, Architecture, Urbanisme', paper delivered at the seminar 'Architectures exportées: transferts, expérimentations, métissages' (Laboratoire Urbama Université de Tours, équipe LAA Ecole d'Architecture de Paris-La Villette et Laboratoire Ladrhaus Ecole d'Architecture de Versailles, 1993).

Béguin, François, *Arabisances: Décor architectural et tracé urbain en Afrique du nord, 1830–1950* (Paris: Bordas Editions, 1993).

Clarence, Perry, *The Neighborhood Unit: A Scheme of Arrangement for the Family Life Community*, Regional Plan of New York, 7 vols (New York: Regional Plan Association, 1929).

Depaule, Jean-Charles and Arnaud, Jean-Luc, *A travers le mur* (Paris: Editions Parenthèses, 1985).

de Tarde, Guillaume, Tarde, 'L'urbanisme aux colonies et dans les pays tropicaux', in *L'urbanisme en Afrique du Nord. Rapport général*, ed. by Jean Royer, 2 vols (Paris: Les éditions de l'urbanisme, 1932), I, 27–31.

Dethier, Jean, 'Soixante ans d'urbanisme au Maroc. L'évolution des idées et des réalisations', *Bulletin Economique et Social du Maroc*, 118–19 (1970), 5–56.

Ecochard, Michel, *Casablanca: Le roman d'une ville* (Paris: Editions de Paris, 1955).

Gaudin, Jean-Pierre, 'Tours et détours coloniaux de l'urbanisme français', *Dossiers des Séminaires Techniques, Territoires et Sociétés*, 4.4 (1988).

Mouline, Said, 'Architecture Métissée et Patrimoine', *Old Cultures in New Worlds, 8th ICOMOS General Assembly and International Symposium Programme Report - Compte rendu* (Washington, DC: US/ICOMOS, 1987), pp. 715–22.

Pinson, Daniel and Zakrani, Mohamed, 'L'adaptation d'un système d'habitat composite: le lotissement économique au Maroc', in *Stratégies urbaines dans les pays en voie de développement: politiques et pratiques sociales en matière d'urbanisme et d'habitat*, ed. by N. Haumont and M. Alain (Paris: L'Harmattan, 1987), pp. 313–27.

4. Taking Ownership of Colonial Heritage in Casablanca

Nezha Alaoui

Introduction

During the period of the French protectorate, various architects in Morocco designed modern residential complexes intended to encourage the local Muslim population's gradual transition towards an urban lifestyle, rooted in traditional customs. Instead, however, inhabitants rapidly transformed these dwellings to create a hybrid habitation, reflecting a cross-cultural mode of life. Despite giving rise to numerous issues, these modifications have enabled residents to assert ownership over their properties, thereby diminishing the remaining vestiges of colonialism.

This chapter aims to demonstrate the significance of these modifications by analysing their impact on families and communities in four of the most extensively altered modernist buildings, located in the outlying districts of Casablanca: Semiramis, Nid d'abeilles and Cité Horizontale. By exploring notions of identity, lifestyle, family and community within the context of Casablanca's modernist architecture, this research provides a nuanced understanding of experimental housing architecture in former colonial territories.

During the modernist era, one of the most symbolic periods in recent architectural history, architects and urban planners implemented mass-housing projects to accommodate the growing shantytown population under French colonial rule. For French architect Michel Ecochard and his team, the buildings constructed in Casablanca 'pour le plus grand nombre' [for the greatest number] were an architectural revolution.

   https://doi.org/10.11647/OBP.0460.04

However, this heritage is still a controversial aspect of the contemporary Moroccan urban landscape, perpetuating debates on perceptions of transformed colonial architectural heritage.

Moreover, the effective application of planning and design tools requires analysis at both the local and global levels. Exploring the complexities of these twentieth-century modernist structures contributes to our understanding of a pioneering system. The implementation of such tools is a crucial unresolved problem for the development of large cities. Furthermore, the buildings under examination offer potential solutions for rethinking fundamental aspects of design in order to export successful architectural principles to foreign countries.

Understanding and assessing Casablanca's modern heritage is an especially delicate task given that these constructions are the work of foreign architects in a colonial context, built to accommodate lower-class migrants and shantytown residents. Nevertheless, the design and construction of these dwellings was a watershed event in the history of modern architecture, widely considered the 'greatest realisation' since Le Corbusier's housing unit.[1] Moreover the Moroccan example is viewed as a testament to the revolutionary rationalisation of modernist theories.

In exploring the origin, current perception and sense of belonging associated with these structures, this study employs an empirical analytical approach, expanding on traditional knowledge and strengthening theoretical foundations. Data collection methods include surveys, interviews, observations and archival research based on both print and online sources. The analysis draws on well-established theoretical perspectives, assessing contradictions in the data to reveal the role of modernist theories in shaping these architectural models. Additionally, it examines inhabitants' appropriation of these dwellings, which drastically transformed their living environment

Unless otherwise stated, this chapter is based on personal fieldwork conducted in July 2015 and June 2018, during visits to four buildings—three in Hay Mohammadi (the Semiramis and Nid d'abeilles buildings as well as a building in the Cité Horizontale residential complex), and one in Sidi Othmane (a component of the Cité Verticale residential complex). Interviews were conducted with four to five families per building,

---

1   Jean-Louis Cohen and Monique Eleb, *Casablanca: Mythes et figures d'une aventure urbaine* (Malkof: Hazan / Casablanca: Belvisi, 1998).

totalling eighteen families. Each family had an average of four members, many with women spanning two or three generations. The interviews, conducted in the Moroccan dialect, lasted approximately thirty minutes. Questions revolved around lifestyle, duration of residency, manner of housing acquisition, and awareness of the building's history.

Fig. 4.1 The current state of a building in the Cité Horizontale of Hay Mohammadi. Author's photograph, 2017, CC BY-NC-ND.

Fig. 4.2. The current state of the Semiramis building. Author's photograph, 2017, CC BY-NC-ND.

Fig. 4.3 The current state of the Nid d'abeilles building. Author's photograph, 2017, CC BY-NC-ND.

Fig. 4.4 The current state of two buildings in the Cité Verticale of Sidi Othmane. Author's photograph, 2017, CC BY-NC-ND.

The chapter is divided into six sections, the first of which presents the necessary urban historical background and projects relevant to the present study. The second section outlines the development of the mass-housing concept, including the design process, results, theories and model. The third section explains various aspects of the inhabitants' modifications, while the fourth section highlights the alterations' impact on the building and the resulting perceptions at the local and international levels. Finally, the chapter situates the architectural and urban approach within its contemporary local and global context and offers concluding insights.

The Historical Urban Background

Soon after his arrival in Morocco in 1912, Louis-Hubert Lyautey, the first Resident General of the French protectorate, designated Casablanca as the main port and economic capital of Morocco. This resulted in an industrial boom that attracted an influx of labourers to the city from the Moroccan countryside.[2]

The arrival of Michel Ecochard on 17 April 1947 was a turning point in the urban history of Casablanca. Appointed as the head of the newly established urbanism and architecture department commissioned by Resident General Eirik Labonne, Ecochard drafted plans between 1946 and 1952 that significantly contrasted with anything that had previously been done in Morocco.[3] In the field of urban planning, Ecochard's work remained a benchmark until the late 1970s.

Until then, the prevailing opinion had been that only individual houses with courtyards were suitable accommodations for the local population. However, the experimentation with new mass-housing theories, coupled with the *tabula rasa* conditions and favourable circumstances of French rule, gave rise to the construction of a modern architecture shaped by local constraints.

The increasing urban density in Casablanca had been a major concern for architects and urban planners for over three decades. Between 1926 and 1947, the population rose by 10% per year as a result of industrialisation. Urbanisation under the protectorate created a significant gap between urban and rural parts of Morocco, as the medina of Casablanca became overcrowded and unable to accommodate new arrivals. Consequently, the first *bidonville,* or shantytown, appeared in the suburbs in the 1930s. Before long, the slums of Ben m'sik and Carrières Centrales housed between 40,000 and 60,000 inhabitants.[4]

---

2   Mathias Gunz, *Casablanca, Morocco the Force of the Everyday* (Zürich: Lars Müller, 2015).

3   Michel Ecochard, *Casablanca: le roman d'une ville* (Paris: Editions de Paris, 1955).

4   Cohen and Eleb, *Casablanca.*

The French sought to create an adapted living space for the local Muslim population at a time when individual houses were considered the only viable option for their accommodation. In this context, Ecochard expanded the original concept of adapted dwellings for Muslims, proposing new solutions such as communal buildings 'for the greatest number', including poor, working-class shantytown residents and rural migrants.[5] These residential complexes were constructed in the suburbs near shantytowns and industrial sites.

Most of the shantytown residents the Housing Department sought to accommodate came from the Atlas Mountains. In devising a suitable solution, the new architects sought inspiration in rural settlements, especially the Kasbahs, diverging from previous architects who drew inspiration exclusively from urban dwellings. The design process was based on a number of studies on the working-class lifestyle,[6] which informed the development of an adapted habitation with insights into the customs, environment and religious practices of the main groups.

Research was also undertaken on traditional Moroccan urban and architectural features in order to inform the construction of dwellings for the Muslim population. Subsequently, the prominent features of the medina, especially grids and structures, were developed. The buildings were positioned one next to the other, resulting in a dense, compact and well-organised medina. Street size varied according to function, from larger streets with many intersections to narrower dead-end alleyways leading to residential clusters.

The Moroccan house, called *dar*, is characterised by specific architectural components and proportions, as detailed in a manuscript by Jean Gallotti.[7] For example, rooms and their openings are arranged around a patio, which is the central courtyard. In referencing these aspects of local architecture, Ecochard and his team expanded their

---

5   Monique Eleb, 'The Concept of Habitat: Ecochard in Morocco', in *Colonial Modern: Aesthetics of the Past, Rebellions for the Future*, ed. by Tom Avermaete, Serhat Karakayali and Marion von Osten (London: Black Dog, 2010), pp. 152–60.

6   Robert Montage, *Naissance du prolétariat marocain. Enquête collective exécutée de 1948 à 1950* (Paris: Peyronnet, 2016); André Adam, *Casablanca: Essai sur la Transformation de la Société Marocaine au Contact de l'Occident* (Paris: Centre National de la Recherche Scientifique, 1968).

7   Jean Gallotti, *Le jardin et la maison arabe au Maroc* (Arles: Actes Sud, 1926).

scope beyond mere decoration and ornamentation, focusing instead on organisation and structure.

The protectorate's ambition with these new constructions was to create an adapted residential space that would encourage the Muslim population's gradual transition to an urban lifestyle through the incorporation of local traditional customs. Ecochard's experimentations were not based solely on previous architectural work but also on personal observations and analysis of the new medina, an approach consistent with modernist principles. In this context, Charlotte Jelidi finds that the buildings adhered to the basic principles defined by the Athens Charter, including economic sustainability and orientation, among others.[8]

The Design Process: Modernism and International Resonance

The modern residential structures in Casablanca reflect the international debate that has characterised the shifts in recent architectural history. Three different camps emerged within the ATBAT-Africa[9] team: Marcel Lods' partisans, Le Corbusier's followers, and Ecochard's young recruits.[10] Conflicting opinions among the architectural team in Morocco indicated a lack of collaboration among its members, who submitted their proposals separately to the CIAM congress.[11] The consideration of the local habits of shantytown residents marked a new phase in collective thinking, as highlighted by CIAM. During the 1953 Aix en Provence Congress, the team highlighted shared opinions on the uniqueness of the urban environment and persuaded a modernist panel of the necessity of incorporating adaptable criteria as an important part of the design process.

---

8   Charlotte Jelidi, 'Hybridités architecturales en Tunisie et au Maroc au temps des protectorats: orientalisme, régionalisme et méditerranéisme', *Architectures au Maroc et en Tunisie à l'époque coloniale* (2009), 42–62, https://shs.hal.science/halshs-00641468

9   ATBAT-Africa was an important architecture firm, established by Marius Boyer, that operated in Morocco during the French protectorate era.

10   Eleb, 'The Concept of Habitat', pp. 152–60.

11   The CIAM (Congrès Internationaux d'Architecture Moderne) were congresses organised to promote dogmatic modernist ideas such as functionalism and rationalisation.

Indeed, the design methods and the tools used by the Groupe des Architectes Modernes Marocains (GAMMA)[12] [Group of Moroccan Modern Architects] posed a challenge to, threatened and contradicted several concepts, principles and values of the modernist movement. The next section will demonstrate how the model developed for the design of the modern mass-housing project for Muslims was revolutionary for its time.

Aligning with a Charter of Habitat project in the early 1950s, based on the Athens Charter, architecture was viewed as a way to gradually enable people to embrace a modern lifestyle, using comfort to encourage certain physical, cultural and social behaviours.[13] Thus, ATBAT's work illustrated the principles and intentions developed during this experimental phase, applying the global modernist vision within local contexts.

Most of the buildings met the social, economic, cultural and geographical requirements of the local environment. For example, the Moroccan climate was a crucial consideration during the design process. Numerous factors such as solar orientation had to be considered given Casablanca's Mediterranean and oceanic climate characterised by mild, humid and often wet winters and hot and dry summers. Consequently, individual buildings were situated on sufficiently spacious plots, aiming to construct simple, well-oriented architectural forms. This created ample space with a suitable distance between facades, optimising sunlight exposure to produce a microclimate through the judicious distribution of volume.[14]

Ideological and social principles also shaped the architects' approach to communal buildings. For example, some designs were inspired by analysis of the old medina's individual houses. The intermediate space introduced by Candilis was intended to ensure residents' privacy with a vertical arrangement of this traditional typology, including reinterpreted patios and chicane entries. Moreover, the spatial adjustment, especially

12   The GAMMA group were modernist architects in Morocco practicing and discussing ways of incorporating global modernist ideas to the Moroccan local context.

13   Tom Avermaete and Maristella Casciato, *Casablanca Chandigarh: Bilans d'une modernisation* (Montreal: CCA, 2013).

14   Cohen and Eleb, *Casablanca*.

in the design of the two-level enclosed patio, took into account religious practices, which will be discussed in greater detail later in the chapter.

The construction of these experimental mass-housing buildings was a groundbreaking development in the international context. However, its underlying principles, rooted in modernist theories, were still intensely debated within the architectural community at the time. This is most aptly illustrated by the example of the debate on the Nid d'abeilles, which gained international exposure in the renowned magazine *l'Architecture d'Aujourd'hui* on 1 December 1954. This publication contributed to the circulation of this model, which challenged precepts considered dogmatic and absolute. Far from merely imitating Western practices, these projects contributed to the renewal of modern architecture worldwide, making their way to foreign countries and enhancing architectural and housing research.

Residential Modifications: Alterations or Improvements?

Soon after the housing projects' completion, the inhabitants modified these residential buildings in ways that preserved their essential structure. This structure, an architectural innovation of the twentieth century, was notably durable, providing a framework within which 'the dreams and necessities of life can express themselves'.[15]

Although contemporary urban architecture in Morocco is still characterised by this concrete post and beam system and block work, numerous alterations can be observed in many modern buildings in Casablanca. This includes the four emblematic buildings examined in this research: the Cité Horizontale of Hay Mohammadi, the Semiramis, the Nid d'abeilles, and the Cité Verticale of Sidi Othmane. These administrative districts were exploratory sites for innovative theoretical approaches, undertaken in Hay Mohammadi by Team 10 (a group consisting of architects such as Georges Candilis and Shadrach Woods, and also of engineers including Henri Piot and Vladimir Bodiansky,

---

15   Avermaete and Casciato, *Casablanca Chandigarh*, p. 165.

among other collaborators), and in Sidi Othmane by André Studer and Jean Hentsch.[16]

The modifications made by inhabitants have been driven by the density of these buildings, which can be classified by two typologies: the Cité Horizontale, an ensemble of low-rise patio houses, and the Cité Verticale, an ensemble of high-rise patio houses.

The Cité Horizontale of Carrières Centrales applies the model of Ecochard's grid. The project was constructed in 1951 on a 100-hectare site intended to accommodate 32,000 shantytown inhabitants.[17] Upon completion of the construction, the Housing Department allocated half of the residences to private developers, sold a quarter to the railway company, and distributed the rest to industries and individuals.[18] However, the area underwent rapid densification, and in less than a decade, the number of houses increased from 1,000 to 3,300.

The modifications made by inhabitants to these single-story mass-housing buildings have included adding upper levels and excrescences, as depicted in Figure 4.5. These heterogeneous elements have transformed the modern urban landscape into a replica of a medina.

As the following examples illustrate, occupants were also able to modify the vertical ensembles. In 1953, Candilis and Woods constructed the Semiramis building near the Cité Horizontale, as well as the Nid d'abeilles building, which was intended for a less religious and conservative population. Both buildings, like the Cité Horizontale, originally belonged to the private developers' companies. They incorporated traditional features such as reinterpreted patios that served as family spaces and gathering areas.[19]

---

16   Marion Von Osten, 'Architecture without Architects: Another Anarchist Approach', *E-flux Journal*, 6 (2009), https://www.e-flux.com/journal/06/61401/architecture-without-architects-another-anarchist-approach/
17   Cohen and Eleb, *Casablanca*.
18   Ibid.
19   Ibid.

Fig. 4.5 The current state of a building in the Cité Horizontale. Author's photograph, 2017, CC BY-NC-ND.

Fig. 4.6 Current state of the Nid d'abeilles building. Author's photograph, 2017, CC BY-NC-ND.

Unlike Semiramis, the Nid d'abeilles featured colourful facades, larger windows and narrower stairs, adopting the architectural style of the South Moroccan Valley. Since then, the buildings have been dramatically transformed, particularly Nid d'abeilles's main facade, which is now unrecognisable, as shown in Figure 4.6.

Another example of vertical ensembles is the Cité Verticale of Sidi Othmane built by architects Hentsch and Studer in two phases in 1953 and 1955. The modern structure is recognisable for its distinctive use of pilotis to support the patios. Due to their low cost, concrete and brick were the primary materials in this construction. Additionally, the apartments were designed with north-south orientation, a characteristic of modern architecture. The ensemble also included a small commercial centre. Unlike the buildings in Carrières Centrales, this project has been subject to minimal alterations.

Quest for Identity

Over a span of fifty years, the studied structures have experienced diverse transformations. The initial inhabitants approached their new, more durable and permanent dwellings with the same principles they had applied to their previous temporary and adaptable shelters. Subsequently, the majority of recent occupants further modified these residences. As one scholar noted, residents transformed the building so extensively through their use of it that it became almost unrecognisable.[20] Alterations to these significant designs, such as vertical extensions of Ecochard's 8x8 grid and expansions on open spaces, have reduced the number of green spaces due to the haphazard construction of commercial units and mosques. This has led to a considerable increase in the density of the residential complex.

The act of dwelling encompasses place-making and the creation of additional value, with a sense of belonging ranked one of the most important values in individual life. In this context, inhabitants' modifications better reflect their needs and are more suited to their way of life. This engagement is a personal contribution, as the appropriation

---

20   Marion Von Osten, 'Displaying the Absent: Exhibiting Transcultural Modernism', in *Cultures of the Curatorial*, ed. by Maria Lind (Berlin: Sternberg Press, 2012), pp. 115–33.

of space involves not just taking control of a place, but also actively contributing to its redefinition and the creation of new meaning.[21] Here, the occupants' notion of intimacy is predominantly determined by culture and religion.

Moreover, in the design of these structures, the architects aimed to influence cultural behaviour and encourage inhabitants to adopt a more progressive lifestyle. This manifested architecturally in large openings and spacious balconies. However, soon after the buildings' completion, modifications to the facades—for example, reducing the size of windows, concealing patios, and raising low walls—embodied the dialectical tension between private and public spaces. Residents made a clear statement in altering the initial design to better fit their needs. They also actively invested in the mass-housing buildings through appropriation, creating additional value, attachment and identity. This action reinforced their profound connections with their dwellings.

This exposes the discrepancy between the model developed by the GAMMA team and the practical space built for the former shantytown inhabitants. In this context, 'the concept of model played a significant and prominent role in some attempts to provide an epistemological foundation for architecture'.[22] However, the theoretical concept underlying the architects' initial intentions was challenged by its practical application. When constructing the residential complexes, the architects sought to adapt to local and social conditions while still providing a widely replicable model. Despite their socially conscious approach, the architects sought to make an international statement. However, this residential model was reshaped by inhabitants through the distortion of grids, the alteration of facades and the modification of floor plans. In these ways, residents actively contributed to exposing the gap between the theorical model and the tangible form of habitation. Beyond mere adaptation, this process of appropriation serves as a practical representation of the inhabitants' needs and aspirations.

---

21 Perla Serfaty-Garzon, 'Dwelling, Place Making and the Experience of Transition and Relocation', in *Festschrift Zum 60 Geburtstag Von Peter Jockush*, ed. by A. Kleinenfen (Kassel: Presses universitaires de Kassel, 1994), pp. 117–34.

22 Filippo Fiandanese, 'Architectural Models: Legacy and Critical Perspectives', *Les Cahiers de la recherche architecturale urbaine et paysagère*, 4 (2019), https://doi. org/10.4000/craup.1885

As a result of these factors, the modernist project was transformed into a unique residential form far removed from the rural-inspired habitations initially envisioned by the architects. This reflects a tangible and realistic confrontation between GAMMA modernist theories and the practical needs of the population. Whether or not these modifications have been successful will be examined in the following section.

The Perception of Colonial Heritage

The numerous modifications have considerably altered the initial design to the extent that they have made the dwellings unsuitable and hazardous to the inhabitants' health. However, Ecochard foresaw some of these unauthorised transformations at an early stage of the project.[23] For example, he anticipated the construction of upper levels, the obstruction of windows, and the conversion of superposed patios into inhabitable rooms. His predictions were based not only on previous scholarship, such as that of Pierre Pelleter and Pierre Mas,[24] but also on his personal observations and analysis of the new medina. Here, the majority of the houses contained one or two storeys, with street-facing windows concealed by closed blinds or stonework. Additionally, the lack of hygiene contrasted with the existing sanitary standards. These very alterations were undertaken in the residential complexes that are the subject of this study, validating Ecochard's apprehensions.

Residents' modifications have exacerbated issues stemming from the initial design, which can be broadly reduced to three main concerns: communication, acoustics and visual privacy. To start with, hallways have become a site of social interactions, which is deemed unacceptable by the majority of Moroccans who prefer greater privacy. Secondly, there has been a reduction in acoustic privacy in the projects, particularly in Semiramis.[25] The numerous modifications implemented over the years have not improved the quality of soundproofing, leaving this problem unresolved.

---

23   Ecochard, *Casablanca*.

24   Pierre Pelleter and Pierre Mas, *L'habitat en nouvelle médina* à Casablanca (Paris: Direction de l'intérieur, 1950).

25   Robert Auzelle, *Technique de l'urbanisme: L'aménagement des agglomérations urbaines* (Paris: Centre National de la Recherche Scientifique, 1953).

Whether the perception of heritage is negative or positive is determined by the historical context. As Peter Van Roosmalen observes, when it comes to colonial heritage, we need to reconsider the tendency to treat it as insignificant or merely a source of shame, embarrassment, or anger.[26] Thus, the study of these residential complexes and structures, which are part of a global yet particular and unique movement, presents an opportunity to appreciate certain tools and design processes. Furthermore, the diversity of styles and features is characterised by the fact that 'each element of this multitude claims its local belonging but also that [and] of a global movement'.[27] In other words, the architects blended local and global influences to create a new practice that, while seemingly ordinary, is highly unique due to its lasting legacy.

These experimentations were followed by the global emergence of mat-building in the late 1950s, with ideological and social principles shaping architects' conception of collaborative buildings. Indeed, this revolutionary form of architecture embodies spatial qualities 'where the functions come to enrich the fabric, and the individual gains new freedoms of action through a new shuffled order, based on interconnection, close knit patterns of association and possibilities for growth, diminution and change'.[28]

In 1961, the theories developed in Morocco provided a basis for evolving residential complexes constructed in Toulouse by Candilis and Wood.[29] These same architects also collaborated with Alexis Josic and Manfred Schiedhelm in designing the Free University of Berlin in 1963. Between 1964 and 1965, Le Corbusier and Guillermo Jullian de Fuente used the same system for the Venice Hospital, incorporating climate control elements into its design. Alison and Peter Smithson's 1968–72

---

26 Peter Van Roosmalen, *Changing Views of Colonial Heritage* 5 (Paris: World Heritage Papers, UNESCO, 2003), pp. 121–28.

27 Laura Verdelli and Daniel Pini, *Planning and Management of Urban and Landscape Heritage; Planification et Gestion du Patrimoine Urbain et Paysager* (Bologna: Bononia University Press, 2012), p. 105.

28 Alison Smithson, *Team 10 Primer* (Cambridge, MA: Massachusetts Institute of Technology Press, 1974), p. 3.

29 Jean-Louis Cohen *et al.*, *Modernity: Promise or Menace* (Kranj Slovenia: Gorenjski Tisl Storitve, 1995).

project, 'Urban Study and Demonstration Mat-Building' fully embraced Arabic traditions, such as patios.[30]

While markedly different from the Moroccan experience, which adhered to the functional segregation highlighted in Le Corbusier's 1933 Athens Charter, each of these examples demonstrates the potential for evolution and change rooted in a strong underlying pattern.

Evolving Perceptions, Identity and Context

Hybridisation and globalisation have played an important role in the formal recognition of twentieth-century heritage in Morocco. In their designs, architects fully embraced Arabic traditions, such as patios, chicane entrances, and spatial distribution patterns.[31] Moreover, hybridisation was inspired by influential theories from around the globe at the time. For example, GAMMA architects were influenced by American concepts such as verticality, characterised by high-rise buildings. Additionally, Jean-Louis Cohen and Monique Eleb noted that Ecochard's plan incorporated the linear city principle developed by foreign architects such as Arturo Soria y Mata from Spain and Nikolai Milioutine from Russia.[32] However, the principles developed on Moroccan territory were later exported and utilised internationally. Projects for American bases were designed by Hentsch and Studer prior to 1956,[33] based on foundational themes used in the buildings of Sidi Othmane

Changing local environments are socio-cultural, geographic and economic aspects of the urban context, which continuously shape buildings' appearance and substance. According to the United Nations Educational, Scientific and Cultural Organization (UNESCO), 'urban growth is transforming the essence of many historic urban areas. Global processes have a deep impact [...] on the perceptions and realities of their inhabitants and users'.[34] Thus, the relationship between physical

---

30   Jaime J. Ferrer Fores, 'Mat Urbanism: Growth and Change', *Projections*, 10 (2006), 3–83.
31   Verdelli and Pini, *Planning and Management*.
32   Jean-Louis Cohen *et al.*, *Modernity*.
33   Cohen and Eleb, *Casablanca*.
34   UNESCO, *Recommendation on the Historic Urban Landscape, Including a Glossary of Definitions* (Paris: UNESCO, 2011), p. 3, https://whc.unesco.org/document/160163

space and its context, particularly between the community and its environment, significantly affects heritage conservation and assessment. UNESCO's Vienna Memorandum highlights the need to focus 'on the impact of contemporary development on the overall urban landscape of heritage significance'.[35]

The changing environment of Casablanca is thus a crucial consideration in the assessment of its twentieth-century heritage. In this large city, urban growth has contributed to the fluidity of economic, social and cultural opportunities for the residential complexes in question. For example, due to the city's expansion, these ensembles have come to occupy a more central, rather than suburban, location. Additionally, the repeated modifications undertaken by inhabitants have temporarily altered these buildings, although these changes may be reversible by further contextual factors. As the urban context evolves, it will continue to transform the city's architecture.

Conclusion

This chapter argues for the use of bold criteria to assess the heritage value of modified modernist residential complexes in Casablanca. After introducing the historical urban context and detailing the emblematic case-study projects, this research has analysed the inhabitants' modifications, including their underlying causes and resulting issues. This analysis has revealed that despite these alterations, the residential ensembles hold considerable value, derived from the modification of a universal yet unique heritage.

The paradox of appropriation lies in the tension between individual identities and universality. This heritage is thus a part of Moroccan history shared by a global community. Moreover, local and intercultural interactions have generated a hybrid product. By adapting their designs to the local environment, the architects demonstrated a deep interest in Moroccan culture. The way this heritage is perceived continues to be shaped by the evolving local landscape, including threats and opportunities emerging from changes in the urban context.

---

35 UNESCO, *Vienna Memorandum 2005: Managing the Historic Urban Landscape* (Paris: UNESCO, 2005), p. 2, https://whc.unesco.org/en/documents/5965

The design and construction of these dwellings marked a watershed moment in the history of modern architecture, with the Moroccan experience considered a testament to the revolutionary rationalisation of modernist theories. In this context, preserving and enhancing these twentieth-century buildings contributes to addressing current urban issues in Morocco. Slums remain a critical problem for the development of large cities, especially Casablanca. The buildings under study, which previously enabled the large-scale relocation of former shantytown residents, could offer potential solutions. The adaptations made by inhabitants likewise present an opportunity to study and optimise these solutions to create a more suitable model. Unfortunately, this task is made increasingly difficult by the deterioration of these buildings.

Thus, the formal recognition and protection of this twentieth-century heritage must be made an urgent priority in order to avoid further damage. The controversial aspect of this heritage could incite efforts to dismiss, demolish or undermine it, particularly for financial motives. However, the preservation of this valuable heritage is crucial, representing 'an opportunity to pass the end of the one-way tie of dependence on colonial production to develop its own, specific or better shared disciplinary approach'.[36] These structures are sites of 'mutual heritage' due to their colonial context and the inhabitants' interventions, which have enabled its integration into the local context. Here, identity and heritage are interdependent notions. Recent heritage reveals the significance of symbolic layers, and without its allegorical value, heritage would merely be inheritance.

Bibliography

Adam, André, *Casablanca: Essai sur la Transformation de la Société Marocaine au Contact de l'Occident* (Paris: Centre national de la recherche scientifique, 1968).

Auzelle, Robert, *Technique de l'urbanisme: L'aménagement des agglomérations urbaines* (Paris: Centre National de la Recherche Scientifique, 1953).

Avermaete, Tom and Casciato, Maristella, *Casablanca Chandigarh: Bilans d'une modernisation* (Montreal: CCA, 2013).

---

36   Verdelli and Pini, *Planning and Management*, p. 75.

Cohen, Jean-Louis *et al.*, *Modernity: Promise or Menace* (Kranj Slovenia: Gorenjski Tisl Storitve, 1995).

Cohen, Jean-Louis, and Eleb, Monique, *Casablanca: Mythes et figures d'une aventure urbaine* (Malkof: Hazan / Casablanca: Belvisi, 1998).

Ecochard, Michel, *Casablanca: Le roman d'une ville* (Paris: Editions de Paris, 1955).

Eleb, Monique, 'The Concept of Habitat: Ecochard in Morocco', in *Colonial Modern: Aesthetics of the Past, Rebellions for the Future*, ed. by Tom Avermaete, Serhat Karakayali and Marion von Osten (London: Black Dog, 2010), pp. 152–60.

Ferrer Fores, Jaime J., 'Mat Urbanism: Growth and Change', *Projections*, 10 (2006), 3–83.

Fiandanese, Filippo, 'Architectural Models: Legacy and Critical Perspectives', *Les Cahiers de la recherche architecturale urbaine et paysagère*, 4 (2019), https://doi.org/10.4000/craup.1885

Gallotti, Jean, *Le jardin et la maison arabe au Maroc* (Arles: Actes Sud, 1926).

Gunz, Mathias, *Casablanca, Morocco the Force of the Everyday* (Zürich: Lars Müller, 2015).

Jelidi, Charlotte, 'Hybridités architecturales en Tunisie et au Maroc au temps des protectorats: orientalisme, régionalisme et méditerranéisme', *Architectures au Maroc et en Tunisie à l'époque coloniale* (2009), 42–62, https://shs.hal.science/halshs-00641468

Montage, Robert, *Naissance du prolétariat marocain. Enquête collective exécutée de 1948 à 1950* (Paris: Peyronnet, 2016).

Pelleter, Pierre and Mas, Pierre, *L'habitat en nouvelle médina* à **Casablanca** (Paris: Direction de l'intérieur, 1950).

Serfaty-Garzon, Perla, 'Dwelling, Place Making and the Experience of Transition and Relocation', in *Festschrift Zum 60 Geburtstag Von Peter Jockush*, ed. by A. Kleinenfen (Kassel: Presses universitaires de Kassel, 1994), pp. 117–34.

Smithson, Alison, *Team 10 Primer* (Cambridge, MA: Massachusetts Institute of Technology Press, 1974).

UNESCO, *Vienna Memorandum 2005: Managing the Historic Urban Landscape* (Paris: UNESCO, 2005), https://whc.unesco.org/en/documents/5965

UNESCO, *Recommendation on the Historic Urban Landscape, Including a Glossary of Definitions* (Paris: UNESCO, 2011), https://whc.unesco.org/document/160163

Van Roosmalen, Peter, *Changing Views of Colonial Heritage 5* (Paris: World Heritage Papers, UNESCO, 2003).

Verdelli, Laura and Pini, Daniel, *Planning and Management of Urban and Landscape Heritage; Planification et Gestion du Patrimoine Urbain et Paysager* (Bologna: Bononia University Press, 2012).

Von Osten, Marion, 'Architecture without Architects: Another Anarchist Approach', *E-flux Journal*, 6 (2009), https://www.e-flux.com/journal/06/61401/architecture-without-architects-another-anarchist-approach/

Von Osten, Marion, 'Displaying the Absent: Exhibiting Transcultural Modernism', in *Cultures of the Curatorial*, ed. by Maria Lind (Berlin: Sternberg Press, 2012), pp. 115–33.

5. Postcolonial Marrakesh: Issues with the Conception and Reception of the Medina

Assia Lamzah

Introduction

Since achieving independence in 1956, Morocco's postcolonial trajectory has been characterised by the ongoing struggle to reconcile its past and traditions with its aspirations for development and modernity. Marrakesh, like all former colonial Moroccan cities, underwent several changes imposed by French architects and planners that reshaped its urban structure. These alterations have had direct and long-lasting consequences for the city's social and urban fabric.

In contemporary Marrakesh, conflicting forces collide, resulting in a chaotic and eclectic urban environment. This complexity has arisen from a multitude of overlapping problems, the majority of which originated under French colonial rule and have gone unaddressed in the decades since independence. Thus far, urban planners and developers have been unable to completely resolve these issues. One of the main challenges facing city managers in Marrakesh today is the management of the city's cultural heritage, accumulated over Morrocco's rich history. This challenge raises questions of how this heritage should be defined and preserved, as well as for whom.

This chapter explores the Marrakesh medina in relation to its colonial past, elucidating how this history shapes the medina's contemporary

 https://doi.org/10.11647/OBP.0460.05

reception and perception. More precisely, it views contemporary Marrakesh as a site of competing group interests and examines how it has been conceptualised according to divergent objectives in various historical and socio-political contexts. The study sheds light on ways that local elites and government actors instrumentalise cultural heritage to reify state power and frame Moroccan identity, either in opposition to or continuity with its colonial legacy.

At the same time, this chapter recognises that for ordinary users, the city and its heritage are more than a mere instrument for the promotion of bureaucratic ideology and national identity. For its citizens and visitors, Marrakesh is a site of everyday life, work, residence, leisure and tourism, accommodating diverse aspirations in highly complex and contested ways.

Thus, this chapter aims to understand what the city's cultural heritage means to its diverse users, focusing specifically on the Marrakesh medina. The data for this study is mainly sourced from structured and unstructured interviews conducted over a decade of research in postcolonial theory and the formation and reception of Moroccan medina space. This research incorporates the perspectives of a range of users and managers of the medina, including officials and non-officials, Moroccans and foreigners, and individuals of varying ages, genders, ethnicities, education levels and socio-economic backgrounds. Additionally, it reflects discussions with NGO representatives, private architects, government officials, state managers and private investors engaged in the medina's heritage management. The insights from these interviews are combined with direct observations focusing on specific aspects of how people interact with the medina space in their daily lives. The objective has been to assemble as diverse a sample of interviewees as possible in order to assess the perceptions of the medina among its various users with the greatest degree of accuracy.

Fully acknowledging the dramatic transformation of everyday life in the postcolonial Marrakesh medina, the intention of this research is neither to romanticise nor celebrate these events. Rather, emphasis is placed on recognising the value and significance of these ongoing changes as a crucial aspect of Marrakesh's self-reinvention. Notably, it is often difficult to definitively discern who is responsible for what or where the boundaries lie between what it is real and what is socially constructed. Nevertheless, this chapter demonstrates that highly tangible assumptions, practices and dynamics are at work in this context. Moreover, actors—whether individual or collective, official or non-official—may not be fully conscious of their own contributions to the medina's social fabric, and none can operate with a complete understanding of the holistic narrative.

Marrakesh and the Cultural Heritage Paradigm

The impact of colonisation and colonial culture on local space and heritage is extremely complex, ambivalent and nuanced. Ian McNiven and Sean Connaughton argue that re-conceptualising heritage sites as 'cultural heritage places represented an important anticolonial step whereby local peoples regained better control of their lives'.[1] Similarly, according to David Lowenthal, it is only when the past has faded away, becoming a 'foreign country', that we begin to mark and commemorate it.[2] Echoing Pierre Nora's observation, it is when we stop experiencing memory spontaneously from within that we begin to 'design memory, to create its external signs and traces, such as monuments and museums and historic buildings'.[3]

From this perspective, the proliferation of external memory markers in the contemporary built environment signals the loss of a more organic cultural memory that supposedly existed in the 'hazy' pre-modern past.[4] In this context, former colonial cities represent a unique and fascinating case study for examining the past as it relates to architectural and urban heritage. However, analysis of these cities must go beyond the vestiges of their relationships with their colonial history. As Simone Abdou Malique argues, we must analyse the ways in which postcolonial African cities are productive, enabling us to see not only the limitations of these spaces but also their potential.[5] Viewing these cities exclusively

---

1   Ian McNiven and Sean Connaughton, 'Cultural Heritage Management and the Colonial Culture', in *Encyclopedia of Global Archaeology,* ed. by Claire Smith (New York: Springer, 2018), pp. 1908–14 (p. 1908).

2   David Lowenthal, *The Past is a Foreign Country* (New York: Cambridge University Press, 1985).

3   Pierre Nora, *Les lieux de Mémoire* (Paris: Gallimard, 1997), p. 37.

4   Kirk Savage, 'The Past in the Present', *Harvard Design Magazine,* 9 (1999), https://www.harvarddesignmagazine.org/articles/the-past-in-the-present/

5   Simone Abdou Malique, *For the City Yet to Come* (Durham, NC: Duke University Press, 2004).

in terms of their colonial and postcolonial relationships often obscures their innovative, modern and resourceful aspects, precluding a fuller understanding of their multifaceted engagement with the wider world.[6]

Today, Marrakesh stands at the heart of this debate, a prime example of a city struggling to reconcile its history and 'authenticity' with its modernist contemporary elements.[7] Marrakesh has long been portrayed and marketed as an exotic, ancient and mysterious city, reminiscent of the romanticism of *One Thousand and One Nights* (also known as *The Arabian Nights*). Paradoxically, it is described by the Moroccan government as a fully modern metropolis with all necessary infrastructure for modern life, including internet cafes, shopping malls, business centres and cyber-parks. Cultural heritage plays an instrumental role in supporting both of these narratives, albeit in different ways.[8]

The Marrakesh medina, a UNESCO World Heritage Site since 1985, is home to approximately 500,000 people, which constitutes 21% of the city's total population. With an area of 640 hectares, it is the largest medina in the Maghreb region. This vast historic urban site preserves all of its medieval features, including its water system, urban facilities, dwellings, souks, *mellah* (Jewish quarters) and working neighbourhoods. Its physical environment and urban structure have been relatively well-preserved and, centrally located within Marrakesh, the medina represents an important residential and commercial centre for the entire city.

Developing a preservation policy for the Marrakesh medina required almost five decades of research and experimentation to devise a strategic approach to this complex urban site. However, many past conservation efforts have failed due to their disregard for the harmony of the medina's broader urban fabric and, in some cases, their reliance on imported strategies ill-suited to the local context. Another factor in the failure of these strategies has been their lack of awareness of local needs and locally developed skills and opportunities.

---

6   Ibid.
7   Assia Lamzah, 'Urban Design and Architecture in the Service of Colonialism in Morocco', *International Journal of Global Environmental Issues Inderscience Enterprises*, 13(2/3/4) (2014), 326–38.
8   Hamid Irbouh, *Art in the Service of Colonialism: French Art Education in Morocco: 1912–1956* (New York: Binghamton University, 2000).

Postcolonial Marrakesh: Issues during Its Conception

After the end of the French protectorate in 1956, the socio-economic gap between Marrakesh's poor and wealthy quarters became entrenched in the societal structure. This was due to zoning policies[9] first introduced by French architect and planner Henri Prost in the 1914 master plan of the city. The French intervention in Marrakech initially led to the creation of the *ville nouvelle*, a modern quarter designed exclusively for French residents. Established next to the precolonial medina, the *ville nouvelle* and the medina shaped one another's perception.[10]

The changes brought about by colonialism in architecture and city planning were abrupt, imposing a radically different ideology through the new urban morphology and management of the built environment. Colonialism produced a dual society in Marrakesh, caught between its traditional pre-modern roots and a modern capitalist-oriented lifestyle. In architecture and heritage management, this manifested in the creation and normalisation of a duality between traditional, pre-modern, supposedly authentic Moroccan and Islamic architecture, and a modern, functional one. Moreover, rapid urbanisation has been among the most dramatic social phenomena marking the end of the colonial era, both in Moroccan cities in general and specifically in Marrakesh. This trend has persisted and continues to shape urban development postcolonial period.[11]

In contemporary Marrakesh, the urban centre, comprising the medina and the *ville nouvelle*, has failed to serve as a major force in the city's economic transformation. Instead, it has highlighted the associated economic shifts and their negative consequences. This is evident in urban sprawl and the emergence of several new quarters, both formal and informal. Additionally, there has been a general deepening of socio-economic disparities in the city, accompanied by an increase in social degradation and poverty in the medina specifically.

Simone's research on African cities exposes the clash between the lived experiences of city residents and unrealistic Western and official

---

9   Janet Abu-Lughod, *Rabat: Urban Apartheid in Morocco* (New York: Princeton University Press, 1980).

10   Quentin Wilbaux, *La médina de Marrakech: Formation et espaces urbains d'une ancienne capitale du Maroc* (Paris: L'Harmattan Editions, 2002).

11   Assia Lamzah, *Colonialism, Architecture and Cultural Heritage: Marrakesh, Morocco* (London: Presses Académiques Francophones, 2018).

governmental visions of urban planning and development.[12] This clash is also apparent in Marrakesh, where government efforts to manage urban development employ procedures and tools inherited from the French, such as the Schéma Directeur d'Aménagement Urbain and the Plan d'Aménagement. These models are based on certain assumptions and paradigms in their attempt to reshape urban life. However, they have ultimately proven impractical as they fail to account for the specificities of the social fabric and the unique patterns and dynamics of urban development in the city.

Similar problems plague urban and architectural heritage preservation. As a site of national and international cultural heritage, the Marrakesh medina struggles to balance its dual role as both a historic built environment that must be preserved for future generations and a living, contemporary space that meets its users' needs. The recent transformation of the medina's royal garden, Arset Moulay Adbesslam, into a cyber-park is an illustrative example of the divergent yet simultaneous ways in which cultural heritage is constructed and presented.

Fig. 5.1 Interior of the Arsat Moulay Abdesslam Garden. Author's photograph, 2021, CC BY-NC-ND.

---

12   Abdou Malique, *For the City Yet to Come.*

This nine-hectare royal garden dates back three centuries to the early reign of the Alawi dynasty. A designated national heritage site, it is one of the few well-preserved testaments to the landscape of pre-colonial Marrakesh and Alawi art and garden design. However, in 2004, the municipality partnered with a leading Moroccan telecommunications firm to transform the garden into a cyber-park (Figure 5.1). The park is visited by medina residents as well as national and international tourists. For locals, it offers a place for men and women to socialise as well as play areas for children, whereas for tourists, it provides high-speed internet connection and cutting-edge GPS technology.

Notably, postcolonial Marrakesh has also inherited many poorly formed structures and social relations from the colonial economy, exacerbating contemporary challenges and handicaps. This is apparent in the medina, which suffers from numerous social, economic, institutional and juridical problems. According to the Moroccan Higher Planning Commission, poverty and unemployment rates are extremely high in the medina compared to other quarters of the city. This indicates the physical degradation of some of the medina's residential districts, where living conditions are often overcrowded and lack sufficient hygiene and security.

Furthermore, there has been a proliferation in the development of unauthorised buildings as a result of growing demand and construction industry inflation. This demand comes from local residents as well as foreigners who choose to live within the medina, either permanently or seasonally, attracted by its charm and the prospect of escape from modern city life. This foreign influx has led to gentrification in the medina, significantly influencing how it is perceived. The Marrakesh medina is among the first in Morocco to experience gentrification, but the social consequences of this process are often underestimated as the medina's foreign population remains below 1,000. However, the social impact of urban gentrification cannot be measured solely on the basis of such figures. As will be discussed later in the chapter, interviews conducted with Marrakeshi residents for this study highlight the significant and complex impact of gentrification on locals' self-perceptions and their perceptions of the medina.

The issues facing the contemporary Marrakesh medina include those inherited from the colonial period as well as those arising from the complexities of its postcolonial urban development. It should be noted that these problems do not affect all parts of the medina equally, nor is the medina uniquely impacted by problems like the significant socio-economic divide in Marrakesh, which affects all quarters of the city.

The government recognises the role of cultural heritage not only in promoting a positive image of Marrakesh and attracting tourists but also, more importantly, in fostering the city's economic development and improving its residential living conditions. Within the Urban Agency, a governmental institution responsible for urban development, a department was created specifically to handle projects within the medina's boundaries, including requests for the construction, modification, demolition or renovation of buildings and sites. This department is overseen by the Ministry of Housing and Urbanism and was formed to address the aforementioned issues facing the medina's built environment.

Despite the government's efforts to overcome these challenges, all initiatives thus far have remained largely technical. However, problems persist on the conceptual and methodological levels in managing the cultural heritage of Marrakesh. Given the conceptual evolution of preservation over time, contemporary Moroccan architects, planners and preservationists must critically examine the history of preservation in order to develop their understanding and stance on critical issues. Additionally, the notion of 'Moroccan modernity' must be clearly defined.

In this context, the following questions merit analysis: Are Moroccan architects, urban planners and preservationists able to effectively represent both themselves and the broader Moroccan populace? Are they capable of defining Moroccan or Marrakeshi architecture? What criteria should guide the selection of Marrakeshi heritage? How can it be preserved in a way that does not compete with Marrakesh's modernity? The purpose of these questions is to deepen our understanding of the mechanisms through which different social and political groups use and present the medina space according to their varying, sometimes conflicting, needs and expectations.

Certain governmental agencies responsible for managing Marrakeshi cultural heritage still perceive it through an Orientalist lens and according to a particular set of political values.[13] Thus, it is not only past Orientalists who held static and stereotypical views of Moroccan

---

13   Mohammed Hamdouni Alami, 'Mimicking Colonial Design: The Rhetoric of Urbanism in Contemporary Morocco', paper presented at an international

architecture, but also some contemporary practitioners and intellectuals, who often seek solutions to contemporary problems in the planning and architectural repertoire of the past.

Mohammed Hamdouni Alami asserts that the French colonial architectural legacy continues to serve as a central source of inspiration for contemporary architectural policy and practice in Morocco.[14] This occurs despite the apparent rejection of this colonial legacy by postcolonial Moroccan architects, who present their urban construction as a return to a 'true identity' rooted in Arab-Islamic cultural traditions. As a private architect in Marrakesh stated, 'My conception [of Marrakech buildings] uses architectonic elements to emphasise our Islamic tradition and to teach it to its users and viewers'. However, as Hamdouni notes, the reproduction of architectural elements from the past can be understood as a form of 'postcolonial self-Orientalization'.[15]

Fig. 5.2 The Royal Theatre of Marrakech. Author's photograph, 2021, CC BY-NC-ND.

---

conference in Rabat about Postcolonial Cities (Mohamed V University, Rabat, Morocco, 2004).
14 Ibid.
15 Ibid.

The recently constructed theatre building in downtown Marrakesh can be considered an example of this 'self-Orientalising' architecture (Figure 5.2). It embodies an architectural nostalgia for an idealised pre-colonial past, with the incorporation of elements such as horseshoe arches and colonial proportions in the doors and windows. These features reflect the Arabisance style more so than a postcolonial architectural rejection of or response to the colonial past, as articulated in the discourse on heritage preservation and architecture in Marrakesh.[16]

The production of this self-Orientalising architecture occurs in a context where some of the medina's preservationists and planners are caught up in a Eurocentric hegemonic discourse which reduces traditional Moroccan architecture to pastiche and picturesque representations. The medina is thus viewed merely as a monument, focusing solely on its aesthetic and structural aspects while neglecting its social, cultural and economic dimensions as a living space. This results in the conceptual separation of the medina, economically and physically, from the rest of the city.

The exclusive management of this heritage by a single social group is another factor reinforcing the conceptualisation of the medina as an isolated urban component and an immutable space that should not be altered. In most cases, cultural heritage serves the interests of the local elite, bolstering their efforts to construct their image in opposition to the Moroccan 'other'. It is highly politicised, with the selection of sites and buildings for preservation dictated by an official agenda to promote universalist cultural tourism. This agenda often does not align with the needs of local communities and reinforces existing class structures. For example, 'Atlas Marrakech', an NGO that works on Jemaa el-Fna plaza and advocates for its preservation as cultural and intangible heritage, is run predominantly by professionals and intellectuals whose interests and perspectives do not necessarily match those of the local population. Inhabitants themselves also have varying perceptions of this space, adding to the complexity of its interpretation and appropriation.

Urban festivals constitute a significant platform for presenting and constructing the image of cities around the world, including Marrakesh.

---

16   For more on the Arabisance style, see François Béguin, *Arabisances: Décor architectural et tracé urbain en Afrique du nord, 1830–1950* (Paris: Bordas Editions, 1993).

The city hosts two major festivals each year that play an important role in presenting the city to the national and international public, shaping their perceptions of the city and defining it as a cultural commodity. The first festival is the International Film Festival of Marrakesh, modelled after the Cannes Film Festival, which takes place every December. The second is the National Festival of Popular Arts, held every August.

These festivals position Marrakesh as a cultural tourism object while also interpreting and informing the city's social order through the reproduction of its dominant political and ideological structures. Additionally, they play an important role in constructing the public image of the city, especially its medina, with economic, social and political consequences for both the city and its population. Both festivals receive official governmental support and are presented as mechanisms of urban revitalisation and development. They are marketed, particularly the film festival, as a means of attracting tourism and private investment, thereby contributing to the city's enhancement and promotion. These ideas are also supported by cultural tourism,[17] giving rise to what Bella Dicks calls 'visitability', which refers to the 'makeover of various kinds of spaces (physical or virtual) so that they actively call out to and invite the attention of visitors'.[18] This serves to objectify and display Marrakeshi culture in a way that makes it accessible to international visitors, leveraging the city's culture for economic and political gain as well as for social control.

The analysis of the ways in which this culture is constructed and presented reveal its role in informing and reinforcing the existing social order, enabling the government and festival organisers to maintain their social privileges and political advantages. Place and space, primarily historic monuments and sites, are instrumental in this process of objectifying the city's culture. As Dicks explains, 'like "consumer goods" that need symbolic associations to become objects of desire [...] places need clear cultural identities to become visitable'.[19] Thus, city promoters and festival organisers transform visitors into 'consumers of illusions',

---

17 Taieb Belghazi, 'Festivalization of Urban Space in Morocco', *Critical Middle Eastern Studies*, 15.1 (2006), 97–107.

18 Bella Dicks, *Culture on Display: The Production of Contemporary Visitability* (London: Oxford University Press, 2003), p. 61.

19 Ibid., p. 61.

drawing extensively on Marrakesh's history and perceived glorious past in the construction of these illusions.

The Postcolonial Marrakesh Medina: Issues with Its Reception

In contemporary Marrakesh, heritage is perceived differently by various users and interest groups. The interviews conducted for this study reveal the diversity of these perceptions, which will be analysed according to two main groups: the government, and local residents.

The Moroccan government is far from a homogeneous entity in terms of how it presents and markets Moroccan cultural heritage, including in Marrakesh. There are divergent strains within the official governmental discourse, reflecting varied perceptions and approaches among the ministries directly engaged in the preservation of the medina's heritage. Thus, the Ministry of Tourism, the Ministry of Culture, the Ministry of Interior and the Ministry of Housing and Urbanism each interpret Marrakesh's heritage from a different perspective and adopt distinct strategies for its management.

In the mid-1990s, the Ministry of Tourism became aware of the need to diversify the tourism industry and initiated a concerted effort to reshape the country's image. This entailed shifting the focus away from natural attractions like the sea and sunny beaches toward cultural tourism assets. Cultural heritage, heavily concentrated in the medinas, constituted an important component of this new image, strategically intended to attract a greater number of visitors to Morocco.

The Ministry of Tourism thus constructed an image of Morocco at large and Marrakesh in particular that catered to the affinities of potential national and international tourists from middle- and upper-class backgrounds, marketing the city as a sunny, vibrant, traditional and exotic destination. However, despite positioning itself as the guardian of cultural heritage sites, this ministry does not possess the financial resources, in comparison to other ministries, to implement its heritage management strategies. Additionally, it lacks updated methodologies and technologies for heritage management and thus continues to rely on relatively outdated approaches.

Furthermore, the ministry's simplistic view of the medina, or what is called 'Islamic architecture', is reflected in its approach to urban design and national architecture, which is problematic in both its mimicry of colonial design and its perpetuation of the 'Orientalist archetype'. This archetype continues to dominate the discourse and practice of urbanism and architecture, reinforcing static notions of the medina as an inward-oriented city with a central mosque and market-bazaar, featuring a network of narrow irregular streets leading to segregated residential quarters.[20] The disconnect between the physical layout and the social, political and economic realities is one of the main limitations of such archetypes.

The Ministry of Interior, responsible for security, views heritage management as chiefly as a means to control population and the medina territory. It is less concerned with the cultural and ideological aspects of management and possess less socio-cultural knowledge of the medina space. Meanwhile, the Ministry of Housing and Urbanism occupies a middle ground, and is the only ministry relatively equipped with the necessary skills and personnel to develop a heritage preservation strategy. However, this strategy must be devised in collaboration with all other governmental departments and ministries related to cultural heritage, as well as intellectuals, researchers, professionals, NGOs and local residents.

Indeed, one of the greatest shortcomings in the contemporary context is the 'by sector' approach adopted by most ministries and departments in the country. This approach risks creating barriers between different stakeholders and thus preventing the formulation of a general vision, which is crucial for any development project.

In evaluating perceptions of the medina among local residents, interviews revealed two main categories based on differing responses to the heightened foreign presence within the walls of the medina. The first group, mainly comprising conservationists and older individuals, opposes this influx, viewing it as a negative influence on traditional values and a disruption to the Islamic way of life that they believe should prevail in the medina. For example, one sixty-two-year-old woman, accompanied by one of her daughters, asked angrily, 'How do you expect me to educate my daughters on Islamic principles of Haya [modesty] with regard to

---

20   For more on this, see Janet Abu Lughod, 'What Is Islamic about a City?', in
     Urbanism in Islam: The Proceedings of the International Conference on Urbanism in Islam
     (Tokyo: Middle Eastern Culture Center in Japan, 1989), pp. 193–218.

dressing and behaviour when they see these half-naked foreign people walking in the medina streets? We did not go to them; they came to us'.

Meanwhile, the second group, composed mainly of young people, responds positively, embracing the influx as an opportunity to interact with foreigners and thereby heighten their engagement with a more modern world. Some in this group express fascination with the newcomers' perceived modern lifestyle, which they emulate in an effort to escape what they view as the outdated traditional way of life currently dominating the medina. For instance, one twenty-six-year-old man said, 'When I meet tourists from Europe and the United States, I feel good because I interact with them in a way to discover their world and hopefully, I will get a chance to visit one of these modern countries'.

These differences are also reflected in the motivations cited by former residents who have sold their homes and move outside the medina. They commonly identify three main reasons for this decision. While some were motivated by economic factors, others either felt that the medina no longer met their lifestyle needs or reported a diminished sense of belonging within the medina space.

For example, one university professor recently relocated from a *riad* passed down in his family through generations to a villa on the outskirts of the city. As he explained, 'I want to raise my children in a house where running water, electricity, an adequate sewage system, and internet are available—a house that is accessible by car'. This echoes the sentiments shared by many medina residents who, although they are reluctant to leave, feel forced to do so because the medina can no longer meet their basic living standards.

Inhabitants also expressed frustration with the lengthy authorisation process required for routine home maintenance or renovations, highlighting one of the main challenges of historic residential areas. Given the medina's cultural significance and unique urban character, it is imperative to preserve its fundamental features, such as narrow streets, urban landmarks and existing infrastructure. Despite potential inconveniences for residents, these elements are integral to the medina's sense of place.

Simultaneously, however, it is also essential to ensure that the population's basic needs are met, including running water, sewage systems, electricity and accessibility (particularly in emergencies). The necessary enhancement of these services constitutes a basic element of accommodation, a process crucial for the sustainable development of urban heritage.

Another factor prompting relocation from the medina is the desire to escape the influx of tourists, especially in residential quarters. This sentiment was predominately expressed by former residents from the middle and upper classes and those with higher levels of education. A forty-five-year-old architect, who moved out of the medina five years ago, stated: 'Having to wait for twenty minutes in the small grocery shop of the quarter every morning to buy a piece of bread was not pleasant. [...] Part of a house of the *derb* [street] where I lived was transformed to a coffee shop and all the customers, mainly foreign tourists, want to have the Moroccan traditional breakfast. They have to come themselves to buy the bread, while the coffee shop offers only black coffee and mint tea'. This intrusion and its disruptive impact on ordinary activities like buying food appears to have weakened residents' sense of belonging within the medina space.

Conclusion

The complex impacts of colonisation and colonial culture on space and local heritage make former colonial cities a fascinating and distinctive case for the study of architectural and urban heritage. This chapter has explored the Marrakesh medina, analysing its relationship with its colonial past as well as how this relationship defines its contemporary reception and perception. The interviews conducted for this study reveal the diverse perceptions of heritage in contemporary Marrakesh among the city's various stakeholders, including government officials, tourists and local residents.

Analysis of these perspectives demonstrates that the conceptualisation and reception of the Marrakesh medina is closely connected to its colonial legacy, which continues to shape both historical and contemporary views. Furthermore, examining how various groups assert their interests in the medina, as well as how divergent objectives shape this living space in relation to its historical and socio-political contexts, holds promise for the development of a preservation strategy for the medina. However, the main challenge of such a strategy lies in reconciling the needs of different users in a way that strengthens the medina's distinct urban and architectural character while allowing for sustainable growth and development.

Bibliography

Abdou Malique, Simone, *For the City Yet to Come* (Durham, NC: Duke University Press, 2004).

Abu-Lughod, Janet, *Rabat: Urban Apartheid in Morocco* (New York: Princeton University Press, 1980).

Abu Lughod, Janet, 'What Is Islamic about a City?', in *Urbanism in Islam: The Proceedings of the International Conference on Urbanism in Islam* (Tokyo: Middle Eastern Culture Center in Japan, 1989), pp. 193–218.

Béguin, François, *Arabisances: Décor architectural et tracé urbain en Afrique du nord, 1830–1950* (Paris: Bordas Editions, 1993).

Belghazi, Taieb, 'Festivalization of Urban Space in Morocco', *Critical Middle Eastern Studies*, 15.1 (2006), 97-107.

Dicks, Bella, *Culture on Display: The Production of Contemporary Visitability* (London: Oxford University Press, 2003).

Hamdouni Alami, Mohammed, 'Mimicking Colonial Design: The Rhetoric of Urbanism in Contemporary Morocco', paper presented at an international conference in Rabat about Postcolonial Cities (Mohamed V University, Rabat, Morocco, 2004).

Irbouh, Hamid, *Art in the Service of Colonialism: French Art Education in Morocco: 1912–1956* (New York: Binghamton University, 2000).

Lamzah, Assia, 'Urban Design and Architecture in the Service of Colonialism in Morocco', *International Journal of Global Environmental Issues Inderscience Enterprises*, 13(2/3/4) (2014), 326–38.

Lamzah, Assia, *Colonialism, Architecture and Cultural Heritage: Marrakesh, Morocco* (London: Presses Académiques Francophones, 2018).

Lowenthal, David, *The Past is a Foreign Country* (New York: Cambridge University Press, 1985).

McNiven, Ian and Connaughton, Sean, 'Cultural Heritage Management and the Colonial Culture', in *Encyclopedia of Global Archaeology*, ed. by Claire Smith (New York: Springer, 2018), pp. 1908–14.

Nora, Pierre, *Les lieux de Mémoire* (Paris: Gallimard, 1997).

Savage, Kirk, 'The Past in the Present', *Harvard Design Magazine*, 9 (1999), https://www.harvarddesignmagazine.org/articles/the-past-in-the-present/

Wilbaux, Quentin, *La médina de Marrakech: Formation et espaces urbains d'une ancienne capitale du Maroc* (Paris: L'Harmattan Editions, 2002).

III. CONTEMPORARY CITIES AND RESIDENTIAL IDENTITIES IN EGYPT

6. Urban Identity in a Polarised Metropolis: Examining the Strengths and Weaknesses of Informal Settlements and Gated Communities in the Greater Cairo Area

Yossr Abouelnour

Introduction

Cairo's urban fabric has undergone rapid transformations in recent years. Repetitive urban patterns have proven unsustainable, giving rise to unfavourable living conditions that undermine the local sense of safety, community and identity. Amidst ongoing debates about which of Cairo's districts offer the greatest potential for community cohesion and identity, this study examines divisive formal and informal planning patterns within the Greater Cairo Area (GCA), investigating two prevailing yet contrasting urban fabrics: gated communities and informal settlements. The juxtaposition of these contexts reveals recurring patterns of urban discourse that are both valued and contested. Moreover, it challenges the presumption of a significant planning dichotomy between the two models, illustrating the successful urban systems, spatial hierarchies and opportunities of each. This comparison underscores the utility of

  https://doi.org/10.11647/OBP.0460.06

integrating the planning methods adopted in these communities and advocates an approach that promotes sustainable, liveable environments and addresses the persistent urban dilemmas faced in both settings.

Housing developments are unique tangible expressions deeply intertwined with notions of 'home' and identity. The patterns and layouts of these urban developments often reflect the values, needs, and aspirations of their inhabitants. Although not always aligning perfectly with residents' ideal visions, the socio-spatial features of these developments can contribute to our understanding of how notions of 'home' are conceptualised by those inhabiting these spaces. This chapter begins with an overview of Cairo's gated communities and informal settlements, outlining the key factors behind their prevalence. It then identifies the unique socio-spatial features and urban patterns of both developments, analysing the positive as well as negative impacts of their resultant urban forms.

The Origins and Proliferation of Two Extremes

As Egypt's capital and most populated city, Cairo is a rich conurbation characterised by coexisting extremes—from luxury cars to humble tuk-tuks (doorless three-wheeled carts), from crooked alleyways to broad asphalt roads, from marble-clad villas to unfinished red-brick exteriors. Nowhere are these contrasts more conspicuous, however, than in the juxtaposition of gated communities and informal settlements.

Informal Areas

Cairo's informal areas, often referred to as *ashwaiyyat*, are existing urban realities that cannot be overlooked due to both their substantial size and population density. These sprawling settlements on the outskirts of neighbourhoods are typically characterised as densely populated 'squatter settlements', lacking legal recognition or privileges. Despite Northern Africa having the lowest slum prevalence in the developing world (15%),[1] informal settlements have become one of the main housing alternatives in Cairo, accommodating the vast majority of

---

1   United Nations Human Settlements Programme (UN-Habitat), *State of the World's Cities 2008/2009: Harmonious Cities* (Nairobi: UN-Habitat, 2008), p. 13.

urban residents. According to 2006 statistics, they were estimated to house more than 65% of the GCA population.[2]

The proliferation of informal settlements (Table 6.1) and urbanisation of agricultural lands in Cairo became noticeable in the mid-twentieth century, particularly following the July 1952 revolution. Factors such as rural-to-urban migration, the reinstatement of strict rental-control laws and the failure of both the government and private sectors to provide adequate affordable housing compelled many low- and middle-income families to turn to informal urbanisation. This habitation model, which mainly took place on agricultural lands on the urban periphery, has continued to expand. Today, there are over one hundred informal developments in the CGA alone,[3] demonstrating that these settlements remain the preferred residential choice for many low- and middle-income families.

Table 6.1 An estimate of the growth of slum populations (*ashwaiyyat*) in Greater Cairo between 1950 and 2000 (GTZ estimates).[4]

Year	Area (square kilometres)	Population (millions)
1950	6.7	0.4
1977	45.7	2.7
1991	106.9	6.3
2000	140.1	8.3

Moreover, the terms 'squatters', 'slums' and 'informal settlements' are often used interchangeably. According to the United Nation's Millennium Development Goals,[5] a 'slum household' is defined as one in which the inhabitants lack of any of the following: 1. access to improved water sources; 2. access to improved sanitation facilities; 3.

---

2   *Cairo's Informal Areas between Urban Challenges and Hidden Potentials*, ed. by Regina Kipper and Marion Fischer (Cairo: German Technical Cooperation, 2009), pp. 17–19.

3   Asef Bayat and Eric Denis, 'Who Is Afraid of Ashwaiyyat? Urban Change and Politics in Egypt', *Environment and Urbanization*, 12.2 (2000), 185–99.

4   United Nations Human Settlements Programme (UN-Habitat), *Cairo: A City in Transition* (Nairobi: UN-Habitat, 2011), p. 18.

5   United Nations, *Tracking Progress towards Inclusive, Safe, Resilient and Sustainable Cities and Human Settlements*, SDG 11 Synthesis Report, High Level Political Forum (Paris: United Nations, 2018), https://uis.unesco.org/sites/default/files/documents/sdg11-synthesis-report-2018-en.pdf, p. 39.

sufficient living area; 4. housing durability; and 5. security of tenure. However, this definition is necessarily limited, encompassing only the negative security, hygiene, and informality aspects while neglecting any potential positive attributes.

Gated Communities

By the late-1990s, Cairo's metropolitan landscape was witnessing radical transformations, with a notable shift towards gated residential developments. Commonly referred to as gated communities, these areas are typically enclosed by walls or fences, with restricted access and privatised public spaces.[6]

Originally envisioned by the government as a solution to housing affordability and density issues, gated communities, unlike *ashwaiyyat*, primarily benefit middle- and high-income populations. In this context, various initiatives by successive governments have helped to facilitate relocation from the inner city, including Abdul Nasser's New Valley governorate and Sadat's satellite towns. This continued during the reign of Hosni Mubarak and persists to this day. As the boundaries between the formal city and the *ashwaiyyat* blurred and their distinctive features faded, the wealthy began to gravitate towards gated communities marketed as 'the cutting edge of a post-metropolitan lifestyle'.[7]

In 2013, approximately 59% of planned housing was directed toward gated communities for Cairo's middle and upper classes, significantly impacting urban and socio-economic development.[8] Given their expansion across Cairo's urban landscape, the implications of these developments are difficult to ignore.

---

6   Edward J. Blakely and Mary Gail Snyder, *Fortress America: Gated Communities in the United States* (Washington, DC: Brookings Institution Press, 1997), p. 2.
7   Eric Denis, 'Cairo as Neoliberal Capital', in *Cairo Cosmopolitan: Politics, Culture, and Urban Space in the New Globalized Middle East*, ed. by Dianne Singerman and Paul Amar (Cairo: AUC Press, 2006), https://hal.science/hal-00379202/document, pp. 47–71.
8   Magda Metwally and Sahar Soliman Abdalla, 'Major Trends of the Gated Communities Development in Egypt: An Approach to Urban Sustainability', paper delivered at the 'International Conference–Privet Urbana Governance and Gated Communities' (University of Brighton 26–28 June 2013).

According to some scholars,[9] media-generated fear of 'the other' is one of many reasons for the prevalence of these remote developments. Often marketed as serene, spatially organised oases, they promise a solution to issues of insecurity, pollution and noise, offering an escape from the perceived chaos and urban decay of the inner cities while catering to idealisations of the American lifestyle.

Patterns, Forms and Fabrics

Successful urban community patterns cannot be designed in 'one fell swoop' but should rather be the result of gradual, incremental and participative efforts to generate appropriate patterns over time.[10]

By focusing on the physical and spatial features and recurring patterns in both Cairene fabrics, this comparative analysis aims to elucidate these unique systems, highlighting both their fragilities and opportunities. The patterns examined include activity and land-use, network and hierarchies of flow, buildings, population density, construction and open space.

Activity and Land-Use Patterns

Mixed-use developments with a sensible variety of programmes are key to ensuring liveable communities.[11] In Cairo's gated communities, there is an evident lack of variety or mixing, with a dominant residential land-use pattern making up 87% of most developments.[12]

Although there is insufficient data on land-use compositions in informal areas and their activity patterns cannot be precisely

---

9   Denis, 'Cairo as Neoliberal Capital', p. 55.

10 Christopher Alexander, Sara Ishikawa and Murray Silverstein, *A Pattern Language: Towns, Buildings, Construction* (Oxford: Oxford University Press, 1977), p. 19.

11 *Livability 101: What Makes a Community Livable?* (Washington, DC: The American Institute of Architects, 2005), pp. 4–54.

12 Islam Ghonimi Ibrahim, Hassan Elzammly and Mohamed Soliman, 'Identification of Gated Communities in Egypt', *Proc. on The Future of Gated Communities, Ministry of Housing and Urban Communities Housing and Building National Research Center* (2011), https://www.bu.edu.eg/portal/uploads/Engineering,%20Shoubra/Architectural%20Engineering/659/publications/Islam%20Ghnemi%20Ibrahim%20 Ghnemi_Identification_of_Gated_Communities_in_Egypt.pdf, pp. 1–13.

quantified, these developments generally offer a more diverse fabric. In a comparison of a gated community and an informal area of a similar scale, we found that the informal area of Bulaq[13] has a highly mixed-use programme, while the Al Jeera compound is comprised of monolithic residential units.

As many services and amenities in informal settlements are established on the basis of need, their distribution is notably efficient and conducive to work-home proximity. However, while many informal areas exhibit a diversity in services, agricultural activities remain dominant, and these communities continue to lack basic facilities such as schools, hospitals and other government services.

Network Patterns and Hierarchies of Flow

There is a relative distinction between public and private routes in informal areas. Public facilities, amenities and services are usually situated on the busier commercial, vehicular and pedestrian streets, while residential streets are generally narrower and shielded from outsiders, allowing them to serve as extensions of homes.[14] Thus, although not deliberately planned, the compactness of these built forms creates walkable neighbourhoods and results in a hierarchical circulation of public, semi-public and private networks. However, the improvised nature of planning, without a solid foundation, means that infrastructure and conventional urban services such as paved roads, water supply, garbage collection and sewer systems are either absent or undertaken informally without proper authorisation.

Additionally, since many informal settlements were built upon former agricultural land, their networks are comprised of long, narrow streets following old drainage canal patterns (Figure 6.2), which poses safety and practicality concerns. Moreover, the prevalence of unregulated transportation services, namely microbuses, can be considered an opportunity as well as challenge. While they create an interconnected

---

13   Heba Allah Essam E. Khalil, AbdelKhalek Ibrahim, Noheir Elgendy and Nahla Makhlouf, 'Could/Should Improving the Urban Climate in Informal Areas of Fast-Growing Cities Be an Integral Part of Upgrading Processes? Cairo Case', *Urban Climate*, 24 (2018), 63–79.

14   Dina K. Shehayeb, 'Advantages of Living in Informal Areas', in *Cairo's Informal Areas Between Urban Challenges and Hidden Potentials*, ed. by Regina Kipper and Marion Fischer (Cairo: German Technical Cooperation, 2009), pp. 35–43.

transportation network and reduce temporal and spatial distances, they also contribute to a higher frequency of vehicular accidents.[15]

Within gated communities, street patterns are predominately inward-oriented, with cul-de-sacs or dead-end roads (Figure 6.1) comprising 62% of their networks.[16] This creates zones or pockets of restricted access within the urban fabric, transforming it into a labyrinth of fragmented, unsustainable urban spaces.[17] This design is intended to establish barriers between the inhabitants themselves as well as between the 'outside world' and the residential community. The resultant circulation pattern contrasts with its surroundings and is disconnected from the rest of the city. Additionally, it discourages the use of alternative modes of transportation and promotes a reliance on private cars, leading to increased greenhouse gas emissions.

AL RABWA   500 m

Fig. 6.1 Street patterns in a gated residential complex (Rabwa) in Cairo. Author's illustration, CC BY-NC-ND.

---

15   Ibid., p. 37.
16   Ibrahim, Elzammly and Soliman, 'Identification of Gated Communities', p. 8.
17   Gunter Meyer, 'Gated Communities in Egypt', in Workshop: Gated Communities–Global Expansion of a New Kind of Settlement, ed. by Georg Glasze and Gunter Meyer (Hamburg: DAVO-Nachrichten, 2000), pp. 17–20.

IMBABA   500 m

Fig. 6.2 Street patterns in an informal settlement (Imbaba). Author's illustration,
CC BY-NC-ND.

Building Patterns and Character

Although informal settlements differ in size, shape and living conditions, they share a common unplanned growth pattern. Dwellings typically vary between one to five rooms, ranging from 41 square metres to 180 square metres in size.[18] Mid-rise family-owned apartment buildings comprising five to seven stories are the most prevalent building prototype, usually constructed from red-brick and cement or reinforced concrete. This variety of building patterns reflects residents' preferences and financial capacities, resulting in unique neighbourhoods with a distinctive urban identity. However, the lack of professional architectural consultation often leads to serious structural, construction and design issues.

---

18   Shehayeb, 'Advantages of Living in Informal Areas', p. 40.

In contrast, the majority of gated communities are comprised of identical units with uniform facades that prioritise aesthetic elements while neglecting passive design principles. These indistinctive design patterns weaken neighbourhood character and often compromise important sustainability measures. While some gated communities, such as Al-Rehab, offer a range of housing prototypes,[19] the majority rely on repetitive models that do not cater to individual preferences. Some offer custom-made homes tailored to residents' needs, such as 'Ruya Residence',[20] but these are still rigidly separated.

Density Patterns

Since Gated communities are designed for middle- and upper-class residents, their spacious prototypes result in low- to medium-density developments. In contrast, Cairo's informal settlements have very high population densities, averaging 38,500 people per square kilometre and sometimes reaching more than 150,000 people per square kilometre.[21] These high densities contribute to neighbourhood vitality, with more 'eyes on the streets'[22] to help maintain public safety and order. According to statistics,[23] the entirety of Sheikh Zayed City has a population density of 2,174 people per square kilometre, while the informal area of Manshiyatnaser has a population density of 46,694 people per square kilometre (Figure 6.3).

---

19 Ahmed Yousry, 'The Privatization of Urban Development in Cairo: Lessons Learned from the Development Experience of Al Rehab Gated Community', paper delivered at the 'International Conference on Developing the New Urban Communities: Policies and Priorities, New Urban Communities Authority (NUCA) and INTA' (2010).

20 Karim Kesseiba, 'Cairo's Gated Communities: Dream Homes or Unified Houses', *Procedia-Social and Behavioral Sciences*, 170 (2015), 728–38.

21 Eric Denis and Marion Séjourné, 'ISIS: Information System for Informal Settlements' (2002), hal-00198975, https://hal.science/hal-00198975/en/, p. 4.

22 Jane Jacobs, *The Death and Life of Great American Cities* (New York: Vintage Books, 1993), p. 54.

23 Thomas Brinkhoff, *Egypt: Greater Cairo*, https://www.citypopulation.de/en/egypt/greatercairo/

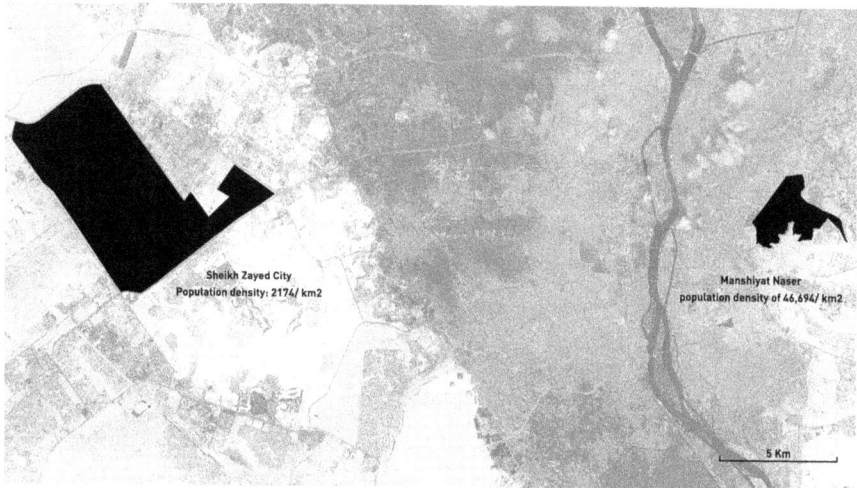

Fig. 6.3 Ground and density population in Sheikh Zayed City and Manshiyat Naser. Author's illustration, based on Google Earth (2020), CC BY-NC-ND.

Construction Patterns

The patterns of construction for these developments follow different approaches. Gated communities adhere to a systemic standardised process, wherein land is purchased from the government by private sector entities or investors. Plans and designs for the proposed projects are then submitted to the New Urban Communities Authority (NUCA) and, upon their approval, infrastructure development begins, followed by construction. The marketing of units and services to be provided takes place simultaneously, prior to the project's realisation.

Informal areas, on the other hand, operate on a self-financed and self-help housing mechanism. The autonomous nature of construction in these areas and their incremental, need-based growth over time gives rise to diversity in household size, building material and overall urban character. The fact that dwellings are typically occupied by the original contractor or builder helps to guarantee at least minimal standards of construction and overall performance. However, this autonomous construction model lacks basic services and infrastructure, the post-facto introduction of which proves to be significantly more expensive than its initial implementation on bare land.

Open-Space Patterns

The presence of green and open spaces is essential in neighbourhoods on account of their environmental, recreational and cultural benefits that directly impact liveability. Unfortunately, modern urban planning in Cairo views green space as a luxury rather than a necessity for urban development.

In informal settlements, public and green spaces are almost non-existent, confined to the limited spaces between buildings (Figure 6.4). Given the soaring population densities, the green space per capita is negligible, with more than half of Cairo's population having access to only 0.5 square metres per person.[24]

While open spaces abound in Cairo's gated communities, as apparent from satellite images and ubiquitous billboards, they are often underutilised and ill-adapted to meet residents' needs. Central green spaces are commonly enclosed by clusters of buildings, and although initially intended as community social hubs, they are generally vacant.

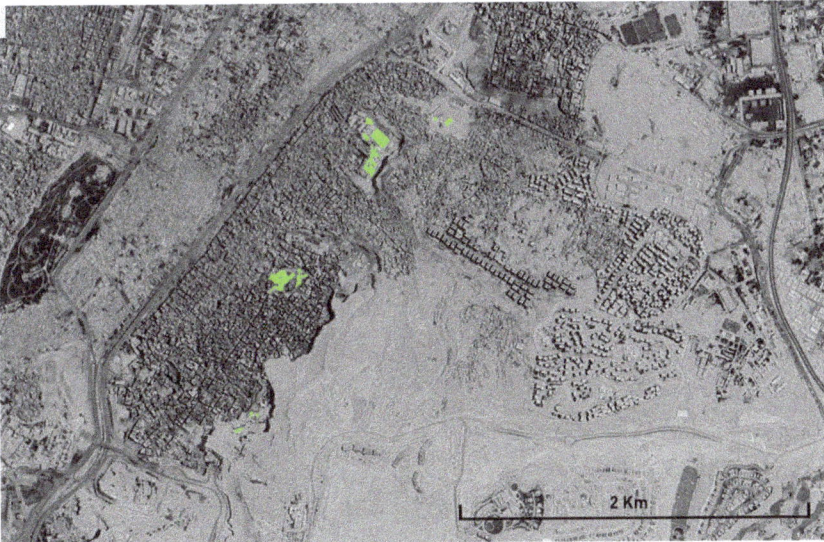

Fig. 6.4 Open green space in Manshiyat Nasser. Author's illustration, based on Google Earth (2020), CC BY-NC-ND.

24   Nezar Kafafy and Yamen Al-Betawi, 'Urban Green Space Benefits and the Pivotal Role of Conservation, Cairo's Case-Egypt' (2011), https://web.archive.org/web/20210708214218/https://eis.hu.edu.jo/deanshipfiles/conf110862020.pdf

Fig. 6.5 Open green space in Sheikh Zayed City. Author's illustration, based on Google Earth (2020), CC BY-NC-ND.

Discussion and Conclusion

The spatial patterns of gated communities and informal settlements do not merely result from the presence or absence of blueprints; rather, they are strongly reinforced by and connected to economic, social and political incentives. Moreover, as a city expands, it becomes fragmented into a patchwork of 'multiple cities that represents increasing social diversification and complexity'.[25]

These urban complexities require proactive policies to identify problems and develop appropriate solutions before they escalate. In this context, laissez-faire policies can encourage the development of disconnected urban fabrics. As Jill Grant and Lindsey Mittelsteadt note,[26] countries that adopt such policies report higher numbers of gated communities.

---

25   Miguel Lacabana and Cecilia Cariola, 'Globalization and Metropolitan Expansion: Residential Strategies and Livelihoods in Caracas and its Periphery', *Environment and Urbanization*, 15.1 (2003), 65–74 (p. 73).

26   Jill Grant and Lindsey Mittelsteadt, 'Types of Gated Communities', *Environment and Planning B: Planning and Design*, 31.6 (2004), 913–30 (p. 926).

Despite the contrasting patterns between gated communities and informal settlements that contribute to Cairo's socio-spatial fragmentation, both fabrics offer valuable insights into planning and spatial organisation strategies.

Informal settlements provide a positive example of grassroots participation in planning. Their adaptability, and customisable residential spaces instil inhabitants with a sense of ownership, fostering feelings of identity and attachment to the built environment. Additionally, the compactness of their built form conserves energy, promotes walkable neighbourhoods and facilitates a convenient home-work proximity.

On the other hand, gated communities offer residents a greater sense of safety and privacy. Abundant green spaces in these areas bolster physical well-being, reduce pollution and improve air quality. Constructed by experienced professionals, they typically do not face the same infrastructure, construction and waste management challenges experienced in informal settlements. Furthermore, they positively impact the surrounding context by upgrading infrastructure and service provision, increasing land value and attracting new services.[27]

Based on this comparison, the following table summarises the urban patterns in gated communities and informal settlements.

Table 6.2 Comparison between urban patterns in gated communities and informal settlements.

Patterns	Main characteristics	
	Informal settlements	Gated communities
Activity and land-use	1. Lack of 'variety' or mixing	2. Highly mixed-use programme
Networks	3. Absence of adequate infrastructure and conventional urban services 4. Interconnected transportation network with shorter temporal and spatial distances	5. Predominately inward oriented 6. Disconnected from the rest of the city
Buildings	7. Different sizes, shapes and living conditions	8. Identical units with unified facades

---

27 Sonia Roitman, 'Gated Communities and the Right to Safety', in *Report of Valladolid: The Right to Security and Safety*, ed. by Rosario del Caz, Mario Rodriguez and Manuel Saravia (Valladolid: Escuela Técnica Superior de Arquitectura de Valladolid, 2004), pp. 187–89.

Density	9. High population densities, e.g.: Manshiyatnaser	10. Low to medium densities, e.g.: Sheikh Zayed City
Construction	11. Self-financed and self-help processes	12. Systemic standardised process requiring approval from government authority
Open space	13. Almost non-existent and limited to the spaces between buildings	14. Exist abundantly but not fully utilised

The comparison of patterns in these developments offers a general if not comprehensive framework for future urban interventions and developments in the GCA. While many gated communities and informal settlements have similar socio-spatial patterns, further research is needed in order to draw generalisable conclusions and develop strategies to maximise urban community benefits. Without a full understanding of existing urban development patterns throughout Cairo, interventions risk adversely affecting existing fabrics and jeopardising urban identity.

In conclusion, this chapter concurs with Christopher Alexander, Sara Ishikawa and Murray Silverstein in emphasising the importance of end-user participation in the development process and its impact on urban liveability:

Towns and buildings will not be able to become alive, unless they are made by all the people in society, and unless these people share a common pattern language, within which to make these buildings, and unless this common pattern language is alive itself.[28]

Bibliography

Alexander, Christopher, Ishikawa, Sara and Silverstein, Murray, *A Pattern Language: Towns, Buildings, Construction* (Oxford: Oxford University Press, 1977).

Bayat, Asef and Denis, Eric, 'Who Is Afraid of Ashwaiyyat? Urban Change and Politics in Egypt', *Environment and Urbanization*, 12.2 (2000), 185–99.

Blakely, Edward J. and Gail Snyder, Mary, *Fortress America: Gated Communities in the United States* (Washington, DC: Brookings Institution Press, 1997).

Brinkhoff, Thomas, *Egypt: Greater Cairo*, https://www.citypopulation.de/en/egypt/greatercairo/

---

28   Alexander, Ishikawa and Silverstein, *A Pattern Language*, p. 10.

Denis, Eric, and Séjourné, Marion, 'ISIS: Information System for Informal Settlements' (2002), hal-00198975, https://hal.science/hal-00198975/en/

Denis, Eric, 'Cairo as Neoliberal Capital', in *Cairo Cosmopolitan: Politics, Culture, and Urban Space in the New Globalized Middle East*, ed. by Dianne Singerman and Paul Amar (Cairo: AUC Press, 2006), https://hal.science/hal-00379202/document

Grant, Jill and Mittelsteadt, Lindsey, 'Types of Gated Communities', *Environment and Planning B: Planning and Design*, 31.6 (2004), 913–30 (p. 926).

Ibrahim, Islam Ghonimi, Elzammly, Hassan and Soliman, Mohamed, 'Identification of Gated Communities in Egypt', *Proc. on The Future of Gated Communities, Ministry of Housing and Urban Communities Housing and Building National Research Center* (2011), https://www.bu.edu.eg/portal/uploads/Engineering,%20Shoubra/Architectural%20Engineering/659/publications/Islam%20Ghnemi%20Ibrahim%20Ghnemi_Identification_of_Gated_Communities_in_Egypt.pdf

Jacobs, Jane, *The Death and Life of Great American Cities* (New York: Vintage Books, 1993).

Kafafy, Nezar, and Al-Betawi, Yamen, 'Urban Green Space Benefits and the Pivotal Role of Conservation, Cairo's Case-Egypt' (2011), https://web.archive.org/web/20210708214218/https://eis.hu.edu.jo/deanshipfiles/conf110862020.pdf

Kesseiba, Karim, 'Cairo's Gated Communities: Dream Homes or Unified Houses', *Procedia-Social and Behavioral Sciences*, 170 (2015), 728–38.

Khalil, Heba Allah Essam E., Ibrahim, AbdelKhalek, Elgendy, Noheir and Makhlouf, Nahla, 'Could/Should Improving the Urban Climate in Informal Areas of Fast-Growing Cities Be an Integral Part of Upgrading Processes? Cairo Case', *Urban Climate*, 24 (2018), 63–79.

Kipper, Regina and Fischer, Marion, *Cairo's Informal Areas between Urban Challenges and Hidden Potentials* (Cairo: German Technical Cooperation, 2009).

Lacabana, Miguel and Cariola, Cecilia, 'Globalization and Metropolitan Expansion: Residential Strategies and Livelihoods in Caracas and its Periphery', *Environment and Urbanization*, 15.1 (2003), 65–74.

Livability 101: What makes a Community Livable? (Washington D.C.: The American Institute of Architects, 2005), 4-54.

Metwally, Magda and Soliman Abdalla, Sahar, 'Major Trends of the Gated Communities Development in Egypt: An Approach to Urban Sustainability', paper delivered at the 'International Conference–Private Urban Governance and Gated Communities' (University of Brighton 26–28 June 2013).

Meyer, Gunter, 'Gated Communities in Egypt', in *Workshop: Gated Communities–Global Expansion of a New Kind of Settlement*, ed. by Georg Glasze and Gunter

Meyer (Hamburg: DAVO-Nachrichten, 2000), pp. 17–20.Roitman, Sonia, 'Gated Communities and the Right to Safety', in *Report of Valladolid: The Right to Security and Safety*, ed. by Rosario del Caz, Mario Rodriguez and Manuel Saravia (Valladolid: Escuela Técnica Superior de Arquitectura de Valladolid, 2004), pp. 187–89.

Shehayeb, Dina K., 'Advantages of Living in Informal Areas', in *Cairo's Informal Areas Between Urban Challenges and Hidden Potentials*, ed. by Regina Kipper and Marion Fischer (Cairo: German Technical Cooperation, 2009), pp. 35–43.

United Nations, *Tracking Progress towards Inclusive, Safe, Resilient and Sustainable Cities and Human Settlements*, SDG 11 Synthesis Report, High Level Political Forum (Paris: United Nations, 2018).

United Nations Human Settlements Programme (UN-Habitat), *State of the World's Cities 2008/2009: Harmonious Cities* (Nairobi: UN-Habitat, 2008).

United Nations Human Settlements Programme (UN-Habitat), *Cairo: A City in Transition* (Nairobi: UN-Habitat, 2011).

Yousry, Ahmed, 'The Privatization of Urban Development in Cairo: Lessons Learned from the Development Experience of Al Rehab Gated Community', paper delivered at the 'International Conference on Developing the New Urban Communities: Policies and Priorities, New Urban Communities Authority (NUCA) and INTA' (2010).

7. Post-Relocation Socio-Economic Study of an Occupational Community in Egypt: Assessing the Social Effects of Relocating the Fishermen Community of El-Mex, Alexandria

Asmaa Abdelhalim[1]

Introduction

The displacement of residents from one location to another is a top-down approach common to many government-led urban renewal projects.[2] Since 1993, this strategy has been used in Egypt to counteract the growth of slums and informal settlements.[3] As a tool, these relocations received the necessary support to achieve political and economic gains, with

---

1   This chapter presents part of the main approach and results of a master's thesis that is a work in progress, with the support of Technische Universität Berlin under the supervision and guidance of Prof. Uwe Jens Walther and research associate, Martin Meyer.

2   Xin Li, Maarten van Ham and Reinout Kleinhans, 'Understanding the Experiences of Relocatees during Forced Relocation in Chinese Urban Restructuring', *Housing, Theory and Society*, 36.3 (2019), 338–58, https://doi.org/10.1080/14036096.2018.151 0432

3   Yahia Shawkat and Amr Abutawila, *Social Justice and the Built Environment: A Map of Egypt* (Cairo: Shadow Ministry of Housing, 2013).

https://doi.org/10.11647/OBP.0460.07

slum removal featuring frequently in presidential election campaigns. However, despite claims that this practice results in a better quality of life for inhabitants, this has not been the norm. In reality, the new housing projects often fail to meet the needs of relocated populations and relocatees frequently are insufficiently compensated for the loss of their original houses.[4]

These discrepancies can be observed in the fishing community of El-Mex, which underwent relocation within the framework of an urban renewal project. One of three main fishing areas in El-Mex, Alexandria is a unique, village-like community rarely found in cities. The fishermen in this neighbourhood form a united community, sharing common values, norms and housing conditions. As an occupational community and urban village, El-Mex constitutes a valuable case study for examining the physical, social and psychological impact of relocation.

Occupational communities are characterised by two key factors: location and people.[5] Within these communities, work-related and non-work-related activities intertwine as individuals with the same professional background interact in social matters and daily life. These people also share similar values and beliefs that influence both their work environment and personal lives.

Occupational communities can also be referred to as 'urban villages', though not all urban villages qualify as occupational communities. Herbert J. Gans described an urban village as a low-rent neighbourhood inhabited by poor residents. These neighbourhoods are often separated from their surroundings by physical or non-physical boundaries, making it easier for residents to identify outsiders. Furthermore, an urban village is defined by a particular quality of social life rather than by its social structure or a specific culture.[6]

In the context of relocation, occupational communities and urban villages are unique case studies and have been the subject of several academic studies. In this research, this literature was analysed to

---

4   Ibid.
5   Edmund Heery and Mike Noon, *Dictionary of Human Resource Management* (Oxford: Oxford University Press, 2008), https://doi.org/10.1093/acref/9780199298761.001.0001
6   Herbert J. Gans, *The Urban Villagers: Group and Class in the Life of Italian-Americans* (New York: The Free Press, 1965).

identify a set of effects experienced by relocatees, which were then used to develop a questionnaire for the relocatees of the El-Mex fishermen village. Drawing upon the author's previous master's research, this chapter thus seeks to verify the presence of the previously investigated effects in the case of the El-Mex fishermen village.

The empirical study focused on applying the insights from the relevant sociological literature to the village. To this end, ten interviews were conducted with El-Mex inhabitants to determine the presence of the identified effects. As a qualitative study, the aim was not to identify a certain trend but to explore the emotions of the inhabitants and their personal experiences of relocation.

Literature Review

In the sociological research on relocation and urban renewal, mental health effects have not been extensively studied.[7] However, one study on social science and mental health in the American urban environment demonstrated how certain statistical research links crime, mental health issues, illnesses and other problems to deteriorated slums. This finding contradicts the arguments of some sociologists that slum clearance is a critical measure impacting the health of inhabitants.[8]

A seminal study on relocation and mental health was undertaken in the mid-twentieth century by Gans in order to discern the effects and results of forced relocation on a community in the West End of Boston.[9] His work emphasised the importance of understanding communities through class, culture and social structure. Thus, he also gathered information regarding lifestyles, values, family structure, daily routines, interactions and attitudes as well as history and background-related information.

Gans clearly defined the urban village as a low-rent neighbourhood, typically—in the American context—occupied by poor European

---

7   Edmund Ramsden and Matthew Smith, 'Remembering the West End: Social
    Science, Mental Health and the American Urban Environment, 1939–1968', *Urban
    History*, 45.1 (2018), 128–49, https://doi.org/10.1017/S0963926817000025
8   Ramsden and Smith, *Remembering the West End.*
9   Gans, *The Urban Villagers.*

migrants and described in ethnic terms based on their countries of origin. He also observed that they tend to separate their community from the outside world by creating physical or non-physical social barriers. Furthermore, his research demonstrated that there is more to these environments than the poor infrastructure or run-down alleys visible to outsiders, arguing that they should not be analysed or renovated based on middle-class needs but based on those of the poor working class.

Gans also described the social ties among the urban villagers as a 'peer group society', based on the commitment and investment in the group over the individual. This concept encompasses a generalised sense of familiarity and warmth rather than the intimacy of one-on-one individual relationships common among the middle class. This notion is reinforced by Marc Fried's concept of the neighbourhood having a 'familistic quality', which manifests in and is sustained by the physical environment. Also examining the post-relocation West End community, Fried found that displacement led to a sense of loss and grief, which he attempted to measure based on various factors analysed across different cases of displacement. Fried also noted that subcultures both explain and are affected by renewal projects, finding that class priorities differ concerning renewal programs. What the middle class considered an upgrade was not necessarily seen as such by other classes.

Moreover, Fried believed that the working and middle classes experience urban environments and physical surroundings differently. The middle class sees an apartment or house as a private space, clearly separated from the street or outer environment. However, the working class extends the concept of home into the street, creating a 'familistic quality' of warmth among family and friends. This identifies the working-class community as a spatial unit rather than just a collection of social relationships.[10]

In his study of relocatee grief, Fried stated that the associated loss has both spatial and social aspects, emphasising the need to examine both to understand the severity of the loss.[11] He noted that feeling at home

---

10   Ramsden and Smith, *Remembering the West End*.
11   Marc Fried, 'Grieving for a Lost Home: Psychological Costs of Relocation', in *Urban Renewal: The Record and the Controversy*, ed. by James Q. Wilson (Harvard,

is central to the sense of belonging, and the stronger the connection between an inhabitant and their environment before relocation, the greater their grief over its loss. He identified three factors to consider when measuring this grief: the spatial factor, the sense of spatial identity, and the social and personal factors.

More specifically, Fried explained that losing the spatial factor affects the individual's sense of continuity by removing a familiar place. The more individuals were engaged with and familiar with the environment, the greater the disruption to their sense of continuity. Furthermore, Fried found that for slum inhabitants, the spatial environment is crucial for social interactions since it is an extension of their homes.[12]

Fried stated that the working class's sense of spatial identity and belonging is tied to a certain place, and thus is severely affected by dislocation. This intersects with place identity, where the spatial element and identity perception are deeply integrated, although social identity can also depend on locations like one's country of origin. Place identity is commonly conceptualised as the emotional link to a place, or place attachment,[13] a theory which P. Van der Graaf used to support the concept of feeling at home. He also identified the same two dimensions of feeling at home: the social dimension of attachment to people and the physical dimension of attachment to place, noting that positive place bonding results in feeling at home.[14] The sense of spatial identity also intersects with group identity, where an individual adopts the identity of larger groups in which they feel they belong, such as a family, ethnicity, social class or profession. Fried stated that a loss in group identity can affect the continuity of the whole group.[15]

Finally, regarding the third factor, Fried explained that it combines pre-location neighbourhood ties and the depth of grief experience by

---

MA: Massachusetts Institute of Technology, 1966), pp. 359–79.

12   Ibid.

13   Fátima Bernardo and José Palma-Oliveira, 'Place Identity, Place Attachment and the Scale of Place: The Impact of Place Salience', *Psyecology*, 4 (2013), 167–79, https://doi.org/10.1080/21711976.2013.10773867

14   P. Van Der Graaf, 'The Lost Emotion : Feeling at Home in Sociology', ISA/RC21 Conference, 22-25th August, Sao Paulom Brazil 2009.

15   Fried, 'Grieving for a Lost Home'.

the individual relocatee. The depth of grief related to personal losses is constant, whether or not spatial factors and identities are involved. Here, Fried concluded that each set of factors contributes to the depth of grief, and any of them can disrupt continuity. Additionally, when continuity is bound to the residential area, its disruption is greater, resulting in higher levels of grief. Understanding the nature of losing a residential environment can lead to better application of relocation practices in both spatial and social aspects.[16]

While previous literature focused on the individual, Barry Wellman described the community as a network. Examining a community of East Yorkers after their integration into the new city of Toronto, he explored the effects of the social division of labour on primary ties and community organisation. He proposed that a geographically bound community can be either lost, saved or liberated. While much sociological work, particularly from the Chicago School, supports the 'lost' argument, some literature argues that the community is saved from restrictive solidarity and primary ties. This 'saved' perspective aligns with certain urban and slum removal strategies, which promote the idea that removing slums can reduce crime rates based on statistical data.[17]

Wellman argued that the 'saved' argument overlooks how social division initially weakened primary ties, which is the basis of the 'lost' argument. He introduced the 'liberated' argument, which highlights the importance of primary ties and distinguishes between having primary ties within the community and having the community as a geographically bound entity. In applying these concepts to the former East Yorker community, Wellman measured their intimate networks. He asked questions about the proximity of intimate persons, whether they were former East Yorkers, and if they were kin. He concluded that while the East Yorkers' community was liberated from solidarity, primary ties continued to exist. However, he noted that the 'liberated'

---

16   Ibid.
17   Barry Wellman, 'The Community Question: The Intimate Networks of East Yorkers', *American Journal of Sociology*, 84.5 (1979), 1201–31, https://www.dhi.ac.uk/san/waysofbeing/data/communities-murphy-wellman-1979a.pdf

argument does not address complex cross-cultural issues or occupational communities.[18]

From the literature, it is evident that relocation affects a community's social, economic and emotional bonds. Social bonds are found in the ties between community members and can be measured similarly to Fried's use of a grief indicator for emotional bonds. Economic bonds relate to rents and jobs. These effects are magnified when there are strong ties between community members and a strong connection between individuals and their physical environment.

Additionally, if the community is working class, their attachment to each other and the environment tends to be stronger. In an occupational community, the ties between individuals may be even more robust. Relocation might liberate individuals from the burden of community solidarity. Alternatively, the community might be saved if it relocates as a whole unit, or it could be lost along with the neighbourhood's aesthetics.

To conclude, the literature identifies several effects of relocation on individuals, including varying levels of grief and the loss of social ties and physical environments. When a community network changes, it can be saved, lost or liberated. In the following case study, these effects will be measured within the occupational community of the El-Mex fishermen village in Alexandria, Egypt.

Case Study

El-Mex is a neighbourhood in the municipality of El-Mex, which is administratively part of the El-Dekhela District in Alexandria, Egypt's second largest city. Figure 7.1 shows the location of this municipality within modern Alexandria. In everyday conversations, El-Mex is strongly associated with a small strip in the district called the 'fishermen village' shown in Figure 7.2 In most previous work, the terms 'El-Mex area' and 'fishermen village' are used interchangeably.

---

18   Ibid.

Fig. 7.1 El-Mex municipality in the city of Alexandria. Author's illustration, based on Google Maps (2021), CC BY-NC-ND.

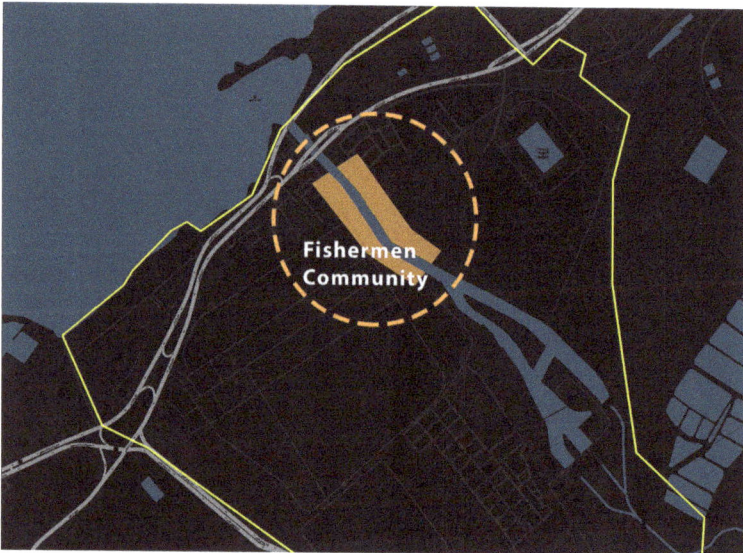

Fig. 7.2 The fishermen community inside the municipality of El-Mex. Author's illustration, based on Google Maps (2021), CC BY-NC-ND.

History and Background

Maps of Alexandria from 1845 show that the El-Mex District was on the city's western border, with traces of a wall built between the Mediterranean Sea and Lake Mariout. Later maps from 1917 indicate that the area was a port, evidenced by the remnants of lighthouses and a fort, which are typically associated with ports in the city.[19]

A 1917 map also shows the existence of the Mahmudiyah Canal drain and El-Mex pumping station, both of which remain landmarks in the district today. The El-Mahmudiyah Canal was established in 1818 with the aim of providing Alexandria with fresh water from the Nile.[20] The 1917 map also depicts a railway extension to El-Mex and a railway bridge over the canal drain, presumably for the transportation of goods. This bridge still stands, and interviews with local inhabitants suggest that it was built by the British and traversed by trains.[21]

Another landmark of the El-Mex District is the so-called lighthouse. It appears on the 1917 map as one of three lighthouses but is referred to as 'a small tower'.[22] Additionally, the early formation of settlements on the banks of the canal is discernible on the 1917 map. These settlements gradually evolved into today's fishermen village,[23] making it the oldest part of the El-Mex District.

The Fishermen Village

Also referred to as El-Mex Bay, the fishermen village is a part of the El-Mex District inhabited by fishermen. Its physical characteristics

---

19   Hiba Hatem, Jihad Ahmed Abu Saif, and Lubna Ali, 'ALEXANDRIA|AL-MAX - Tadamun' (17 December 2019), *Tadamun*, https://www.tadamun.co/?post_type= city&p=10645&lang=en&lang=en; Centre d'Etudes Alexandrines, https:// www.cealex.org/

20   Nada Adel, Asmaa AlGaredly, and Hamed Gamal, 'El-Mex: The Alexandrian Venice, from Negligence to Eviction', *ECESR : Egyptian Center for Economic & Social Rights* (2016), https://ecesr.org/%d8%a7%d9%84%d9%85%d9%83%d8%b3/

21   Interviews with the inhabitants made by Samar Baiomy in 2018 and 2019 for her project 'Revive Memories'. The author interviewed Baiomy in 2020. Hatem, Abu Saif and Ali, 'ALEXANDRIA|AL-MAX'.

22   Ibid., and Centre d'Etudes Alexandrines, https://www.cealex.org/

23   Hatem, Abu Saif and Ali, 'ALEXANDRIA|AL-MAX'.

contributed to making fishing the primary occupation in the village since the establishment of the first settlements. Most inhabitants worked either as fishermen or in related capacities such as making fishing nets, selling fish in the El-Mex market, or working as carriers. This profession was passed down through generations, just as land and houses were inherited.[24]

This fishermen village was one of three main fishing communities in Alexandria, along with the Abu Qir community in the east and Bahary near the city centre. The village had two to three rows of houses on each canal bank, all overlooking the water. Each house had two doors—one facing the street and one opening onto the water, where there was a fishing boat.[25] In 2007, the *Alsharq Alawsat* newspaper published an article describing the fishermen village as an 'Eastern Venice' due to its resemblance to the Italian city, and the term has been widely used ever since.[26]

Administratively, El-Mex Bay falls under the General Authority for Fish Resources Development (GAFRD), which is part of the Ministry of Agriculture and Land Reclamation. Consequently, the houses in the fishermen village are owned by the GAFRD.[27] However, in 2017, when an eviction notice was issued and the inhabitants protested, the district's general secretary declared the land to be owned by the Ministry of Water Resources and Irrigation, the entity responsible for purifying the canal after the evacuation.[28] Moreover, residents of houses around the canal are required by law to pay property tax as well as a rent to the GAFRD, which varies by area but does not exceed 60 EGP per year (around 6 EUR at the time the reference of the information was recorded).

24   Adel, AlGaredly and Gamal, 'El-Mex: The Alexandrian Venice'.
25   Marwa Kamel El-Sayed, 'Community-Driven Urban Development in Informal Settlements in Developing Countries' (thesis, Alexandria University, 2018).
26   Abdallah Daif (projects' coordinator for the Gudran Association for Art and Development, years 2001–17), interviewed by the author, 28 July 2020.
27   Adel, AlGaredly and Gamal, 'El-Mex: The Alexandrian Venice'.
28   Jacqueline Mounir, 'Residents of "Tolombat Al-Max" in Alexandria Object to the New Housing' (8 December 2017), *Al Youm7*, https://tinyurl.com/2a8dpckd

Fig. 7.3 The fishermen village before the relocation. Photograph by Samar Baiomy, 2017, CC BY-NC-ND.

The Relocation

In 1998, the first decree to demolish the fishermen village was issued.[29] This decree was annulled in 2006 when the inhabitants protested against being relocated 14 kilometres away from the El-Mex District.[30] However, Abdallah Daif explained that what was perceived by the media as a demonstration was actually an artistic installation, part of community development activities organised by Gudran—an association registered with the Ministry of Social Solidarity that worked in the El-Mex fishermen village from 2000 to 2018. Daif added that during the installation, a government informant requested that they 'stop what [they]'re doing', as the decree had been annulled.[31]

---

29   Interview with Abdallah Daif (2020).
30   Adel, AlGaredly and Gamal, 'El-Mex: The Alexandrian Venice'.
31   Interview with Abdallah Daif (2020).

According to Khaled Seddiq, the CEO of the Informal Settlements Development Fund (ISDF), the fishermen village in El-Mex is classified as a 'grade two' on their national map.[32] This means that the area is considered 'life threatening' and its inhabitants need to be relocated to state-owned housing units. Alternatively, residents could receive financial compensation for their dwellings, use existing or temporary housing units, be provided with land for the construction of new houses, or be granted rent allowances for a period of time.[33]

In 2011, a cooperation agreement was signed between the ISDF and the governorate of Alexandria with the aim of developing the El-Mex area by building housing projects in the district and other areas affected by relocation, including the fishermen village. The project later received its first funding instalment per Decree 73/2015, which adopted the draft of the project.[34] The project was envisioned as a new community for the fishermen of El-Mex, comprising eight mixed-use apartment buildings with 160 housing units and 14 shops. In 2018, the governor of Alexandria announced that the project would have nine buildings with 215 units, each measuring 63 square metres.[35]

However, in a 2016 interview conducted for socio-economic research on the area,[36] an inhabitant stated that the housing project was intended not for the fishermen village but for an adjacent area in El-Mex called Tolombat. Hence, the development project was renamed the Tolombat El-Mex Housing project. The inhabitant added that the announcement that the new project was for both areas came later and explained that this project was based on four decrees, but it was unclear which one was being implemented. Ultimately, the fishermen village was mapped three times—in 2013, 2015 and 2016, according to one inhabitant.[37] During this process, the survey committee inspected all of the houses and entered every room.

In December 2018, the inhabitants were informed that they were to evacuate within one week and move to the newly constructed apartments,

---

32   Sayed Mohamed and Amgad Amer, '"Slum Development" Alexandria Will Be Free of Slums by the End of This Year' (2 March 2018), *AlBawaba News*, https://albawabhnews.com/2969794

33   El-Sayed, 'Community-Driven Urban Development'.

34   Adel, AlGaredly and Gamal, 'El-Mex: The Alexandrian Venice'.

35   Mounir, 'Residents of "Tolombat Al-Max"'.

36   Adel, AlGaredly and Gamal, 'El-Mex: The Alexandrian Venice'.

37   Ibid.

where the monthly rent would be 200 EGP (9.8 EUR at the time, 10.9 EUR now). One resident highlighted the substantial increase in expenses and explained that, as fishermen, they could not afford these rental prices.[38] Other problems also arose: some houses were not included in the survey, and the request for a port to store and protect fishing boats prior to the relocation was denied. This prompted a demonstration, with residents refusing to move until their needs were met.

Officials explained that the new apartment buildings had been built on state land and thus rent had to be collected. Further, the governor of Alexandria announced that this was the first phase of the initiative, with a second phase planned to relocate an additional 96 units, and that a port was being constructed for the fishing boats.[39] He also stated that the government was committed to moving residents with prior notice and that the relocation was necessary and in the best interests of the inhabitants. Additionally, the district's general secretary claimed that they were merely executing the evacuation, which was mandated by the Ministry of Agriculture and Land Reclamation.

Fig. 7.4 The demolishing of the east bank after stage 1 of relocation. Photograph by Samar Baiomy, 2018, CC BY-NC-ND.

---

38   Mounir, 'Residents of "Tolombat Al-Max"'.
39   Ibid.

Fig. 7.5 The demolishing of the west bank after the second and final stage of relocation. Photograph by Samar Baiomy, 2020, CC BY-NC-ND.

By the end of December 2018, the east bank had received a one-week evacuation notice and was evacuated in March 2019. The west bank remained inhabited for longer but was completely evacuated by October 2019.[40]

Results

Based on the literature, the effects of the relocation on the fishermen community were analysed according to four factors: the physical loss of their environment, emotional grief, the personal ties among residents and the network within the community.

First, it is important to identify the fishermen village as a community of urban villagers. It constitutes an urban village not only because it is nominally a 'village' situated in an urban area but also because of the homogeneous social life resembling that of an ethnic community. Additionally, the fishermen community is economically impoverished

---

40   Jacqueline Mounir, 'After 4 Months of Faltering ... Alexandria Begins to Transfer the People of El-Max Moat to New Housing' (2 March 2018).

and remains vulnerable to the housing market. Previous research and observations also indicate that the fishermen village was a closed community with its own culture, economic system and social structure, and thus difficult to penetrate.[41]

Like the community examined by Gans, the fishermen village was relocated from a dilapidated area categorised as a slum. Another trait distinguishing the residents as urban villagers, according to previous research, is their minimal concern for their housing conditions beyond basic shelter and security. Home repairs and upgrades were not viewed as a high priority as their sense of home extended to the entire neighbourhood.

In addition to being a community of urban villagers, the fishermen village was also an occupational community. Inhabitants identified strongly with the fishing profession and shared similar values in both their workplace and living environment. Their daily work heightened their attachment to the environment and the neighbourhood, which served as both a home and a workplace, deepening their spatial connection. Their group identity also featured prominently in their professional values and norms, exemplified by statements such as 'we are fishermen, we will not deceive you'. This demonstrates a profound connection with their environment, including both a physical relationship and an emotional bond tied to their identity.

It is commonly assumed that because their collective identity is closely tied to their environment, such a group may struggle to maintain its cohesive identity after relocation. However, in the case of the fishermen village, the entire group was relocated together, which may have contributed to the continuity of the group, according to the reviewed literature. Nevertheless, the emotional grief associated with the move is likely considerable.

When studying the case of the fishermen village, the focus should be on the spatial factor and identity, since the loss of social and personal relations was less severe. However, changes in the urban fabric and unit design created a separation among the inhabitants, causing them distress. Previously, residents would stroll through the neighbourhood and stay updated on their neighbours' lives simply by passing open

---

41   El-Sayed, 'Community-Driven Urban Development'.

doors. In their new apartments, they are behind closed doors and no longer able to do so. Additionally, interviews revealed a deep desire for balconies, which may seem like a luxury but is actually a familiar extension of the home into the external environment, as observed by Fried.[42] Thus, while their primary ties still exist, their conversations and daily check-ins on one another have become less frequent as the new apartments have forced them to adapt to a new lifestyle.

The community, as a network of shared experiences and mutual support among its members, was examined to determine whether the community has been lost, saved, or liberated by relocation. In this context, the interviewees expressed great sadness over no longer sharing as much of their daily troubles and experiences with one another, which they previously enjoyed. Although the relocation of the community to a single building within a compound limited the loss of their primary ties, the preliminary interviews suggested that personal relations were disrupted in some cases by the relocation process itself. Certain relocatees felt it was unfair that those from three-storey houses were relocated to apartments similar in size to those from one-storey houses. Yet, this did not discourage the community from offering support to one another based on their values and beliefs. For example, when a pregnant community member could not afford rent or medical delivery expenses, the community pooled money to cover the cost of her delivery charges and took her to the hospital. This demonstrates that the community still maintains strong internal solidarity.

As for their professional occupation, the disruption in continuity is due not only to the loss of a sense of identity but also to the fact that some experienced the theft of their fishing equipment as they no longer had storage rooms like they previously had in their houses. Additionally, the dock intended to accommodate their boats is not properly designed to meet their needs. The interviewed fishermen doubt the port's capacity to withstand the elements over time, which is likely to result in wind damage to their boats. These concerns led two of the interviewed fishermen to quit their jobs and find other employment—one for commission and the other as a driver—because fishing no longer sustains them. Families

---

42   Fried, 'Grieving for a Lost Home'.

that used to teach their children fishing as a future career have stopped doing so, as it is no longer perceived as a guaranteed job.

However, relocation is not the sole cause of these impacts. Officials prohibit fishing for prolonged periods during the year, typically without prior notice. Fishing permits are becoming more difficult to obtain and to apply for. The renewal process is also uncertain and can take up to several month, during which time fishermen are not allowed to fish. These restrictions, combined with the relocation, have negatively affected the fishermen's access to water and ability to do their job. Consequently, one fisherman chose to sell his equipment, purchase an apartment and contribute to his daughter's marriage expenses. He now sells fish from other fishermen in the market.

Moreover, while the levels of grief among the relocatees vary, the distress caused by losing their homes is high. When recounting the stories of their relocation, most show severe signs of grief, often tearing up and speaking with cracking voices. The same emotions arise when they are asked if they witnessed the demolition of their homes. They share stories of being physically pulled away from their houses during the demolition, unwilling to let go of their homes even after the relocation. When shown pictures of houses before the demolition, they can easily identify whose house is in the picture. If it is their own, it brings back many memories of the forced relocation and the decree. While it should be noted that people may romanticise their past, it is important to acknowledge the emotions of these fishermen.

Their grief was also evident during interviews when they discussed their profession. Many expressed the potential need to find alternative employment in the near future, as they are barely able to get by on fishing incomes. One fisherman, crying, stated: 'The people who took our land do not care about us and do not care if we live or die, and you know what, I wish I would die and leave everything to them. I wish I would have died and not witnessed all this'. This profound level of grief was not found in the urban sociology literature examined earlier in this chapter.

As previously mentioned, while not all these effects are solely the result of the relocation, it does play a major role. Economic factors have made it difficult for the fishermen to afford their new dwellings. Furthermore, their stability and familiarity has been disrupted in addition to the restrictions imposed on their fishing work. The designs of the new buildings and insufficient compensation provided for the former homes have also contributed to the high levels of grief and community disruption. Thus, while relocating the community as a whole had its benefits, greater inclusion of the affected residents and increased participation would have been advantageous for both sides. The relocatees would have benefitted from a project that better reflected the needs they voiced, and the government would have benefitted from using participation as a means to deliver better-perceived development projects in the future.

Conclusion

This chapter examined the effects of relocation on the occupational community of El-Mex fishermen village, showing that the relocatees suffer from similar effects observed in other relocation contexts. Despite efforts to maintain their network and collective identity, the community experiences high levels of grief, and some former fishermen are abandoning their occupation. The discussion indicates that these effects are not solely caused by relocation but result from various factors, including new housing and dock designs, and the economic status of the relocatees.

The chapter also touched briefly upon possible actions to help the inhabitants cope with their grief over their lost jobs and homes and adapt to a new and unfamiliar housing system. Adapting and upgrading commonly used spaces to benefit the community members are possible solutions. However, further exploration of potential solutions is needed.

Bibliography

Adel, Nada, AlGaredly, Asmaa and Gamal, Hamed, 'El-Mex: The Alexandrian Venice, from Negligence to Eviction', *ECESR : Egyptian Center for Economic & Social Rights* (2016), https://ecesr.org/%d8%a7%d9%84%d9%85%d9%83%d8%b3/

Bernardo, Fátima and Palma-Oliveira, José, 'Place Identity, Place Attachment and the Scale of Place: The Impact of Place Salience', *Psyecology*, 4 (2013), 167–79, https://doi.org/10.1080/21711976.2013.10773867

Centre d'Etudes Alexandrines, https://www.cealex.org/

El-Sayed, Marwa Kamel, 'Community-Driven Urban Development in Informal Settlements in Developing Countries' (thesis, Alexandria University, 2018).

Fried, Marc, 'Grieving for a Lost Home: Psychological Costs of Relocation', in *Urban Renewal: The Record and the Controversy*, ed. by James Q. Wilson (Harvard, MA: Massachusetts Institute of Technology, 1966), pp. 359–79.

Gans, Herbert J., *The Urban Villagers: Group and Class in the Life of Italian-Americans* (New York: The Free Press, 1965).

Hatem, Hiba, Abu Saif, Jihad Ahmed and Ali, Lubna, 'ALEXANDRIA|AL-MAX - Tadamun' (17 December 2019), *Tadamun*, https://www.tadamun.co/?post_type=city&p=10645&lang=en&lang=en

Heery, Edmund and Noon, Mike, *Dictionary of Human Resource Management* (Oxford: Oxford University Press, 2008), https://doi.org/10.1093/acref/9780199298761.001.0001

Li, Xin, van Ham, Maarten and Kleinhans, Reinout, 'Understanding the Experiences of Relocatees during Forced Relocation in Chinese Urban Restructuring', *Housing, Theory and Society*, 36.3 (2019), 338–58, https://doi.org/10.1080/14036096.2018.1510432

Mohamed, Sayed and Amer, Amgad, '"Slum Development" Alexandria Will Be Free of Slums by the End of This Year' (2 March 2018), *AlBawaba News*, https://albawabhnews.com/2969794

Mounir, Jacqueline, 'Residents of "Tolombat Al-Max" in Alexandria Object to the New Housing' (8 December 2017), *Al Youm7*, https://tinyurl.com/2a8dpckd

Mounir, Jaqueline, 'After 4 Months of Faltering ... Alexandria Begins to Transfer the People of El-Max Moat to New Housing' (2 March 2018).

Ramsden, Edmund and Smith, Matthew, 'Remembering the West End: Social Science, Mental Health and the American Urban Environment, 1939–1968', *Urban History*, 45.1 (2018), 128–49, https://doi.org/10.1017/S0963926817000025

Shawkat, Yahia and Abutawila, Amr, *Social Justice and the Built Environment: A Map of Egypt* (Cairo: Shadow Ministry of Housing, 2013).

Van Der Graaf, 'The Lost Emotion : Feeling at Home in Sociology', ISA/RC21 Conference, 22-25th August, Sao Paulom Brazil 2009.

Wellman, Barry, 'The Community Question: The Intimate Networks of East Yorkers', *American Journal of Sociology*, 84.5 (1979), 1201–31, https://www.dhi.ac.uk/san/waysofbeing/data/communities-murphy-wellman-1979a.pdf

IV. METROPOLITAN CITIES AND RESIDENTIAL FACADES IN IRAN AND TUNISIA

8. A Comparative Study of Residential Facades in Tehran and Iranian Architectural Principles: Challenges and Strategies

Honey Fadaie[1]

Introduction

Facades play a significant role in defining the architectural identity of buildings. As the primary exterior face of the building, they are the most visible expression of the structure's ascribed meaning, which is perceived differently from various perspectives.[2] Citizens visually assess building facades, forming mental impressions that influence their individual perceptions. A well-designed urban facade can play an important social role, fostering a community's sense of place, orienting their activities and even enhancing collective memories and group communication.[3] The visual comfort of citizens is a key parameter of facade design,

---

1   The author began her studies on Persian gardens in 2008 at the Department of
     Architecture, Roudehen Branch, Islamic Azad University (RIAU), Roudehen, Iran.
2   Hafezeh Poordehghan, Azadeh Shahcheraghi and Seyed Mostafa Mokhtabad,
     'Evaluation and Analysis of the Theoretical Principles of Describable Housing
     According to the Opinions of Citizens', *Journal of Housing and Rural Environment*, 38
     (2019), 81–96.
3   Anahita Zarif Pour Langrodi, Fariba Alborzi and Jamalodin Soheili, 'Explaining
     the Role of Urban Views in Creating Placing Attachment for Citizens (Case Study:
     Tehran Residential Views)', *Journal of Research and Urban Planning*, 20 (2020),
     217–32.

    https://doi.org/10.11647/OBP.0460.08

encompassing elements such as light, colour, environmental quality and physical quality. However, when these components are improperly implemented, it can lead to discord and anxiety in daily urban life.[4]

In Iran, a harmony has historically existed within most major cities, which maintained their natural image through the use of local construction materials and specific colour palettes and designs. Today, however, Iranian cities are plagued by obvious construction and urban planning issues, manifest in buildings that do not reflect local culture, customs, climate and historic urban fabrics.[5] This chapter examines the metropolitan area of Tehran, identifying existing problems associated with designing residential building facades and strategies to ensure their compatibility with the principles and criteria of Iranian architecture.

Tehran has twenty-two districts, encompassing a multitude of facades that are often inconsistent, lacking identity and visually unappealing. For this reason, in 2014, the municipality of Tehran established a Facade Committee in each district, with the aim of aligning urban facades with the principles of Iranian architecture. The main objectives of these committees are to study facade features, provide necessary instruction on facade design and monitor the implementation of designs according to national architectural parameters. The establishment of these committees is thus rooted in the need to create spaces that align with Iranian historical and cultural identity and the desired image of the metropolis.

Given the visual prominence of facades in architecture, a clear method for their design and understanding is essential, particularly in the case of historical buildings.[6] In many metropolitan areas around the world, special design criteria and guidelines govern the city's visual and physical aspects. Art, architecture and urban planning experts have analysed these criteria at the architectural and urban scale, especially in historical contexts. Moreover, they have criticised modern urban

---

4   Hafezeh Pourdehghan, Azadeh Shahcheraghi, Seyed Mostafa Mokhtabad and Hamid Majedi, 'Evaluating Visual Preferences of Architect and People toward Housing Facades, Using Multidimensional Scaling Analysis (MDS)', *International Journal of Space Ontology*, 4 (2017), 75–85.

5   Sepideh Masoudinejad and Zeynab Aliyas, 'Investigating the Components of Facade Aesthetic and its Effect on Urban Identity', paper presented at the 'International Conference on Civil Engineering, Architecture and Urban Management in Iran' (Tehran, 2017).

6   Mansur Sefatgol, 'Rethinking the Safavid Iran', *Journal of Asian and African Studies*, 72 (2006), 5–17.

planning and its impact on historical contexts, notably at the 19th UNESCO Summit in Nairobi in 1976.

Acknowledging the global consensus on the imperative of preserving local cultural heritage values, this research utilises the principles of traditional Iranian architecture as an analytical framework to examine the criteria and performance of facade committees in the metropolitan area of Tehran. The study employs a descriptive-analytical method, drawing upon both archival research and fieldwork conducted as a scientific member of the facade committees in Districts 9 and 12 between 2014 and 2018.

Following an overview of Tehran's urban landscape and contemporary challenges, the chapter reviews the main elements of facades and factors in their effective design. The next section outlines the five key principles of traditional Iranian architecture and their application to facade design. Subsequent sections explore the criteria and activities of Tehran's facade committees as well as the operational challenges they encounter in the assessment and enhancement process. Finally, the chapter evaluates ten selected facades that have been approved by these committees, analysing their compliance with traditional Iranian architectural principles.

Tehran's Urban Landscape and Its Contemporary Challenges

The metropolitan area of Tehran is located in northern Iran, on the southern slopes of the Alborz Mountains and bordered by the Dasht-e-Kavir Desert to the south. According to the oldest historical records, Tehran's origins date back to before the eighth century, when it was a village with dense orchards of fruit trees.

Tehran first gained prominence as a city in the sixteenth century under the Safavid dynasty, which ruled as one of the most influential powers from 1501 to 1736. Grounded in Iran's traditional administrative system, the political structure of the Safavid Empire was initially shaped by Iranian culture and later became the source of a new type of Iranian identity.[7] Many Iranian cities were developed during this period, including Qazvin, Isfahan and Tehran, in which the reigning Shah took

---

7   Ibid.

a particular interest. Noting the region's abundant streams, favourable hunting grounds and lush orchards, he ordered a fortification with four gates built around the city, encircling a multitude of buildings.

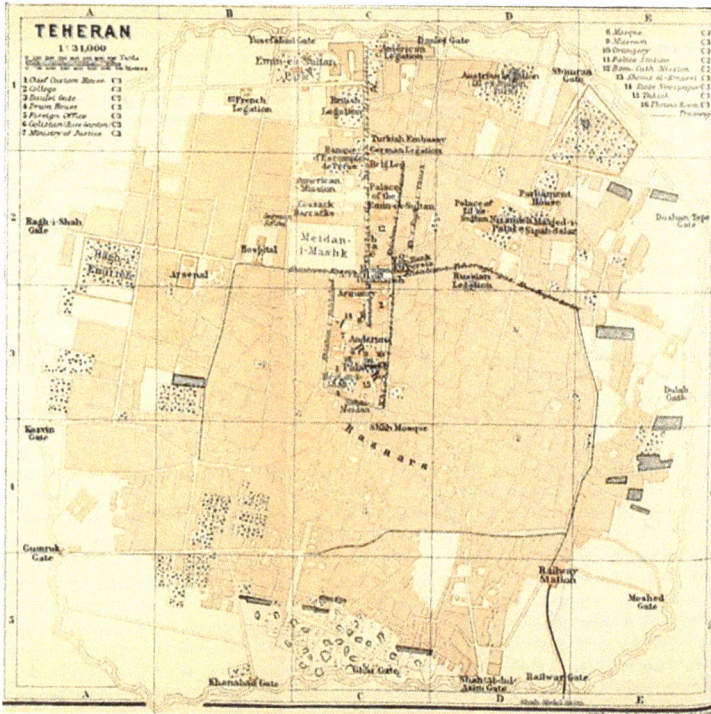

Fig. 8.1 Tehran's development across history, map of Tehran in the early twentieth century. Photograph by Karl Baedeker (1914), Wikimedia, https://commons.wikimedia.org/wiki/File:1914_Tehran_map_byBaedeker.png, public domain.

In 1794, the ruling Qajar dynasty selected Tehran as the Iranian capital, commencing extensive development and construction project. This entailed the removal of old fortifications and the construction of new neighbourhoods, which marked the beginning of an important era in Tehran's urban development.

Another notable turning point came in the 1930s, when modernist trends began to transform the image and structure of Tehran. Many of the city's old neighbourhoods were demolished in order to make way for new buildings and streets constructed in the modern style.

Today, Tehran encompasses an area of 751 square kilometres and is home to a population of approximately 8,700,000 people, making it

Iran's largest and most populous metropolitan area. The city is divided into twenty-two districts, each with distinct economic, cultural and climatic characteristics.[8]

Factors such as extensive immigration, unchecked urban expansion, construction lacking logical design, and imitation of Western architectural styles, especially in building facades, have led to a variety of issues in contemporary Tehran, including the city's symbolic and visual pollution. Symbolic pollution refers to disturbances in the understanding of urban elements, while visual pollution denotes disturbances in the visual landscape, which can manifest in building forms and their constituent elements. This includes urban facades, which may be poorly maintained or exhibit inconsistences in construction materials or colour schemes.[9]

Fig. 8.2 Tehran skyline image: Visual disturbance in urban landscape. Photograph by Amir Pashaei (2019), Wikimedia, https://commons.wikimedia.org/wiki/File:Tehran_in_a_clean_day.jpg, CC BY-SA 4.0.

One example of visual pollution in Tehran is the use of classical facades emulating ancient Greek and Roman architecture in residential buildings, especially in the city's affluent districts. For roughly two decades, these facades have been widely considered acceptable in residential construction despite their complete lack of cultural connection to traditional Iranian architecture. Furthermore, the high cost of stone-cutting and the detrimental economic, cultural and visual impact on the urban landscape has not deterred their use in either the northern regions or, more recently, the southern regions of Tehran.[10]

To address such problems, strategies must be devised for consolidating Tehran's urban aesthetic and halting this destructive process. This

---

8   Ali Madanipour, 'Tehran, National Capital, Iran' (9 April 2025), *Britannica*, https://www.britannica.com/place/Tehran
9   Kevin Lynch, *The Image of the City* (Cambridge, MA: MIT Press, 1960).
10   Mehdi Daryani, *The Principles of Facade Design* (Tehran: Avalo Akhar, 2014).

requires an understanding of both facade components and the principles of Iranian architecture, which will be discussed in the present chapter.

Facade Elements and Effective Design

As the primary exterior component and public face of a building, the facade typically includes the building's main entrance and boasts its most ornate architectural features.[11] Its structure is comprised of elements known as facade constituents, encompassing functional as well as aesthetic components.[12] The most important elements of nearly all residential facades include entrances, materials, openings, ledges (such as balconies) and the skyline.[13]

While people often assess the quality of a house based on the quality of its observable facade, it is important to recognise that the identity of a residential facade is contingent upon its neighbouring buildings and the wider urban context. In other words, the character of street space as a corridor can only be identified through the continuity of its facades.[14] Thus, each facade is a constituent element of the urban space, contributing to its overall structure. For example, within the ensemble of city facades along a street or square, an individual facade may lack symmetry or equilibrium in isolation but, when considered in conjunction with adjacent facades, contribute to the harmony of the overall visual composition.[15]

According to Hafezeh Poordehghan, Azadeh Shahcheraghi and Seyed Mostafa Mokhtabad, urban structure is dynamic, with city formation determined by various factors beyond merely material aspects.[16] Cultural, social and functional parameters can all affect the composition of a given urban landscape. Moreover, scholars like Anahita Zarif Pour Langrodi, Fariba Alborzi and Jamalodin Soheili assert that

11   City of Richmond Department of Urban Planning & Development Review, 'Facade Design Guide' (2013), https://www.rva.gov/sites/default/files/2023-06/PDR%20-%20Aaron%20Bond%20-%20FIP%20Design%20Guide%20FINAL.pdf
12   Rob Krier, *Elements of Architecture* (London: Academy Editions, 1992).
13   Akbar Mokhtarpour, Simin Heydarian and Ftemeh Moslehabadi, *Cityscape, with an Approach to Standards and Principles* (Tehran: Honare-Memari, 2016).
14   Alireza Sadeghi, Elaheh Mousavi, Sarvineh Baghi and Zahra Khodaee, 'Utilizing Iranian-Islamic Approach in the Analysis and Improvement Process of the Quality of Urban Facades', *Journal of Iranian Architecture and Urbanism*, 2 (2019), 69–84.
15   Ibid.
16   Poordehghan, Shahcheraghi and Mokhtabad, 'Evaluation and Analysis'.

the spatial cohesion of a facade hinges on factors such as its coordination with the site and adjacent structures, the dynamics of solid surfaces and voids (e.g., terraces), climate adaptation, aesthetic considerations and appropriate colour schemes and materials.[17]

Thus, the key parameters for evaluating facade design can be generally categorised into physical, functional, aesthetic and climatic components. Each of these components has its own criteria, with some instances of overlap across parameters (Table 8.1).

Table 8.1 Facade constituent components.[18]

Facade constituent components	Criteria and characteristics
Physical	Climate and environment Contextualism Visual proportion Cultural parameters View Transparency Durability Relationship between form and function Flexibility Sense of richness Vitality
Functional	Civil laws (urban management, supervision) Accessibility Variety of activities
Aesthetic	Vitality Flexibility Diversity Historical identity Sense of richness Visual proportions Having natural factors
Climatic	Coordination with the site Climatic strategies Ecosystem preservation

17   Zarif Pour Langrodi, Alborzi and Soheili, 'Explaining the Role', pp. 217–32.
18   Akram Khodamipoor, Hoessein Zabihi and Seyed Majid Mofidi Shemirani, 'Evaluation of Components Influential on Promotion of Landscape Identity of Architecture of Contemporary View', *Journal of Research and Urban Planning*, 4111 (2020), 197–214.

Traditional Iranian Architectural Principles and Their Application in Facade Design

There are various theories on the aesthetics and features of Iranian architecture across different historical eras and geographical regions. One framework widely recognised by scholars in this field is the 'Five principles of Iranian architecture',[19] developed by Iranian architectural historian Mohamad Karim Pirnya. This framework identifies the defining principles of traditional Iranian architectural design as human scale, purposefulness, introversion, self-sufficiency and structure.

This section summarises these principles as outlined by Pirnya and, drawing on the paper 'Utilizing Iranian-Islamic Approach in the Analysis and Improvement Process of the Quality of Urban Facades',[20] elaborates their application in facade design.

1. Human Scale

Traditional Iranian architecture exhibits a human orientation, with structural dimensions tailored to human use and comfort. Other characteristics of this principle include the avoidance of personalisation with simple designs as well as the coordination of buildings within the broader urban fabric.

Fig. 8.3 The neighbourhood and human scale in the old urban fabric of Yazd, Iran. Photograph by Vanalste (2003), Wikimedia, https://commons.wikimedia.org/wiki/File:Yazd,_Iran_Old_City_June_2003_MvA.jpg, CC BY-SA 3.0.

---

19   Mohamad Karim Pirnya, *Recognition of Iranian Architecture Styles* (Tehran: Soroush Danesh, 2001).

20   Yaghoub Peyvastehgar, Ali Akbar Heidari and Motahareh Eslami, 'Recognition of the Pyrnia's Five Principles in the Iranian Traditional Home and its Analysis Based on Islamic Sources', *Journal of Iranian-Islamic City Studies*, 27 (2017), 51–66.

The application of the principle to facade design entails considering human size, perspective, comfort and needs in the design process.

The urban fabric of Yazd, Iran (Figure 8.3) exemplifies simplicity in the urban fabric and the avoidance of personalisation. The simplicity and legibility of the facades, considering the skyline, entrance specificities and dimensions, are among the features corresponding to the principle of 'human scale'.

2. Purposefulness

The principle of purposefulness refers to the avoidance of extravagance and superfluous ornamentation. Iranian architecture is traditionally minimalist with an emphasis on utility, so that even its decorative elements have functional aspects.

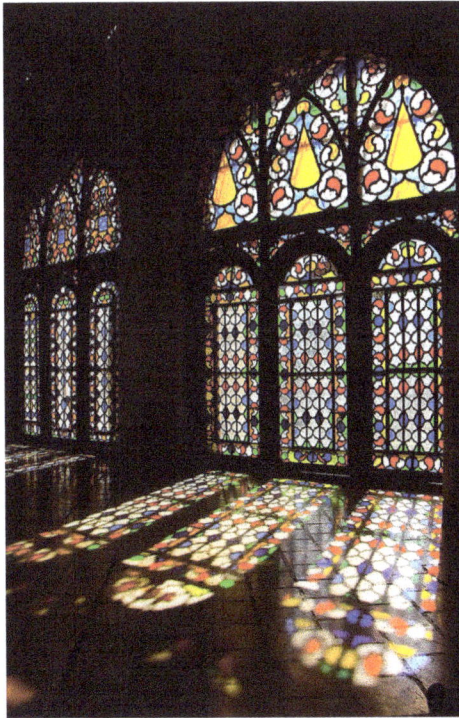

Fig. 8.4 Stained glass facade of the Kazemi house in Tehran, Iran. Photograph by Masoud Mohebbi (2019), Wikimedia, https://upload.wikimedia.org/wikipedia/commons/b/bf/NO.3030-1%D8%B9%D9%85%D8%A7%D8%B1%D8%AA_%DA%A9%D8%A7%D8%B8%D9%85%DB%8C_03.jpg.

In terms of facade design, this principle is embodied in simplicity, favouring relatively homogeneous building materials over costlier alternatives in the construction of external facades.

This principle is embodied in the use of stained glass within a facade (Figure 8.4), which is not only aesthetically appealing but also functions to mitigate solar radiation.

3. Introversion

In most regions, traditional Iranian architecture is characterised by introverted layouts. This is particularly evident in traditional houses, which are spatially organised around a central courtyard. This layout is mainly a reflection of climatic considerations as well as an overarching cultural concern for privacy.

Fig. 8.5 Central organisation around courtyard, Tabtabei house, Kashan, Iran. Author's photograph, 2011, CC BY-NC-ND.

Introversion through the central organisation of space around a courtyard can be seen in the example of this traditional Iranian house, where facade design is oriented around a central courtyard (Figure 8.5).

4. Self-Sufficiency

Iranian architects traditionally believed in utilising locally sourced materials, which are not only easily prepared and cost effective but also compatible with regional environmental conditions. Thus, the principle of self-sufficiency promotes convenience and sustainability through the use of domestic resources.

In the design of Iranian facades, this principle encompasses the use of domestic materials, primarily brick and stone, and the creative incorporation of traditional forms and products. Adherence to this principle reflects environmental awareness and the adaptation to local geographical conditions as well as a respect for local beliefs, traditions and customs.

Fig. 8.6 Local material use in traditional brick facade of the Kazemi house, Tehran, Iran. Photograph by Sepideh Sadafi (2014), Wikimedia, https://commons.wikimedia.org/wiki/File:%D9%86%D9%85%D8%A7%DB%8C_%D8%A8%DB%8C%D8%B1%D9%88%D9%86%DB%8C_%D8%B9%D9%85%D8%A7%D8%B1%D8%AA.jpg#.

This traditional Iranian house (Figure 8.6) exemplifies self-sufficiency, as its exterior facade is composed of brick, a local material commonly used in the construction of traditional Iranian houses.

5. Structure

The structural principle in traditional Iranian architecture has several components, including the integration of structure and ornamentation, the use of modular grids, symmetry and equilibrium, and proportionality in the scale of the building.

In facade design, this principle manifests in harmony among the various dimensions of the visual composition through the congruity and proportionality of facade components.

Fig. 8.7 The modular proportion in traditional Iranian facade of the Borojerdiha House, Kashan, Iran. Author's photograph, 2015, CC BY-NC-ND.

This principle is exemplified in the Borojerdiha House in Kashan (Figure 8.7), which exhibits symmetry and equilibrium in the design of its facade.

Design Criteria and Facade Committee Operations

In 2014, the Tehran municipal organisation established facade committees across its twenty-two districts in order to harmonise the city's facades, particularly those of residential buildings, with Iranian architectural principles. Each of these district committees is composed of two faculty members specialising in architecture and urban design, a municipal representative, the district's deputy mayor, a city council member and a member of the Tehran Construction Engineering Organization. To achieve the stated goals, Tehran Municipality has compiled a set of guidelines titled 'Rules and Regulations for Facade Design', which has been made available to the facade committees. This document categorises the rules and criteria for the residential sector into three main categories: prohibitions, requirements and recommendations. Through this framework, they address the most critical features of facades, as outlined in Table 8.2.

Table 8.2 Rules and criteria for designing residential facades in metropolitan Tehran.[21]

Criteria	Description of criteria
Prohibitions	Refrain from using all-glass or all-metal facades.
	Avoid unconventional and heterogeneous colours in facades.
	Limit the use of multiple materials in facades to a maximum of four.
	Do not use unconventional and unfamiliar processes in design and construction.
Requirements	Use durable materials in the vicinity of the building to prevent erosion and contamination of the facade.
	Coordinate the main colour of the facade with that of neighbouring buildings.
	Conceal the discontinuous seam between two buildings with suitable facade materials.
Recommendations	Avoid using multiple colours on the facade surface.
	Use washable materials on the ground floor to maintain facade appearance.
	Utilise brick, cement, stone or a combination of these materials for the facade.
	Coordinate the design form of the facade with neighbouring buildings.

The rules and regulations in Table 8.2 apply to all of Tehran's twenty-two districts, where their implementation is mandatory. Given Tehran's

---

21   Archive of the Tehran Municipality Facade Committee.

considerable size and the diversity of climatic, economic and cultural conditions across different areas, certain specific criteria governing the dimensions of historical-cultural background, context and climate are necessary to accommodate the unique circumstances of each district. These criteria are compiled in Table 8.3.

Table 8.3 Rules and criteria for facade design based on identity features.[22]

Identity aspect	Explanation of facade design regulations
Cultural and historical background	Avoid incorporating elements of Western architectural comfort into the facade.
	Ensure facades promote tranquillity and respect for neighbours' rights, including views and sunlight access.
	Avoid using symbols contrary to national and religious culture, such as sculptures or Greek and Roman elements.
Physical context and site	Ensure facade harmonises with local identity and natural surroundings.
	Coordinate building dimensions with adjacent facades.
	Create visual cohesion with horizontal lines of urban facades.
	Design adjacent building facades to complement the main facade.
	Ensure that the facade's main material is recognisable among other materials.
	Incorporate the main colour of the environment into the facade in its historical context.
Climatic conditions	Align size, location and orientation of openings with heat and ventilation requirements for comfort.
	Consider local wind direction when designing inlets.
	Limit the area of openings in the facade to less than 21% of the total infrastructure area for optimal energy and sunlight use.
	Design skyline to align with climatic characteristics of the site, such as pitched roofs and domes.
	Use deep entrances for high buildings with entrance halls connected to windward areas.
	Ensure wind speed at ground level, especially in passageways of high or single buildings, do not exceed the comfort limit.
	Avoid creating visual disturbance for adjacent buildings with the facade.

22   Archive of the Tehran Municipality Facade Committee.

Tables 8.2 and 8.3 demonstrate that the choice of materials has a significant impact on the form and visual quality of facades. Among the committee-approved materials, brick and stone are particularly common throughout most regions of Iran. Brick has long been one of the most readily available building materials throughout Iran's architectural history and continues to be widely used in contemporary construction. As Akbar Mokhtarpour, Simin Baba Heydarian and Fatemeh Moslehabadiand observe, 'brick has no limitation in form, texture, materials and performance, because it is flexible, durable, inexpensive, and easy to work with'.[23] In addition, it can be prepared at different times and places. With the discovery of stone mines in Iran and the consequent popularisation of high-rise buildings in the 1960s, the implementation of stone facades became common. The most important advantages of stone materials are non-absorption of dust, variety in colours and materials, moisture resistance, fast implementation, abundance and availability, high durability and strength, thermal insulation and low maintenance costs.

Challenges Facing Facade Committees

Before providing an overview of the facade committees' performance, it is necessary to highlight the challenges they face in evaluating and approving facades. The most significant problems relating to the assessment and enhancement of facade quality are detailed below.

Sound architecture requires careful attention to both the plan and the facade during the design process. However, in Tehran, the presentation of facade designs to committees takes place after the approval of architectural plans by the municipality. In other words, building plans are formulated and approved before the consideration of facades, demonstrating an undervaluation of the facade's significance as a structural component. This issue imposes severe limitations on improving the design quality of facades.

The regulations provided for facade design are the same in all districts, except for the few cases already described (Table 8.3). However,

---

23   Mokhtarpour, Heydarian and Moslehabadi, *Cityscape*, p. 108.

in the metropolitan area of Tehran, each district has its own architectural context, climatic features and economic conditions that should be considered in the design and analysis of the facade. For example, District 1, located on the slopes of the northern Alborz Mountains, has a temperate climate and is inhabited by wealthier residents. In contrast, southern and western districts like Districts 9 and 18 exhibit greater levels of poverty. Moreover, District 12 is home to Tehran's old urban fabric and historical quarters, necessitating special attention in the design of its buildings.

Although evaluating the visual preferences of architects and the general public reveals diverse perspectives on residential building facades, designers have increasingly prioritised the desires of clients, especially in wealthy areas, at the expense of architectural principles and specialised views. As a result, many of the facades reviewed by the committee lack both Iranian identity and architectural standards. This poses considerable challenges between committee members and clients.

Comparative Study of Approved Facades and Their Alignment with Iranian Architectural Principles

Given the substantial number facades in the metropolis of Tehran, it is impossible to review and evaluate all of them in this chapter. For this reason, areas with similar residential fabrics have been excluded from the study, focusing instead on ten residential facades from distinctive districts that have been approved by the committees. These facades have been evaluated based on their compatibility with the five principles of Iranian architecture, the results of which are presented in Table 8.4, where black squares indicate compliance with a principle while white squares indicate non-compliance.

Table 8.4 Evaluation of approved facades by the committees. Author's photographs and illustrations, 2018, CC BY-NC-ND.

District	Picture of facade	Features approved by the facade committees	Principles of traditional Iranian architecture				
			Human scale	Avoiding inefficacy	Introversion	Self-sufficiency	Structure
1		Use of brick as the main materials of the old buildings of the region. Use of solid and void spaces. Combination of facades taken from small cubes in coordination with the slope and old buildings of the region.	■	■	□	■	■
1		The use of stone and brick, two common materials in Iran, as a modular network.	□	■	□	■	■
2		Horizontal elongation due to narrow width of the ten-storey buildings. Rhythm and variety.	□	■	□	□	■
6		Use of brick and stone materials. Use of warm colours for the vitality of the building. Maintenance of privacy through concealing the interior of the building.	□	■	■	■	□
8		Use of light colours in harmony with adjacent facades. Consideration of human scale. Use of a modular grid. Combination of form with light and shadow.	■	■	□	■	■

9	Horizontal elongation due to narrow width. Comparison with the division of the adjacent facades. Use of stone in accordance with the adjacent facades.	■	■	□	■	■
9	Balance in the use of materials (stone and brick). Use of materials similar to adjacent buildings. Continuity among building facades.	■	■	□	■	■
9	Simplicity, symmetry and equilibrium. Use of stone (main material of surrounding buildings). Use of a single material due to the narrow width of the building.	■	■	□	■	■
10	Innovative use of traditional Iranian materials (bricks) without the use of mortar.	■	■	□	■	■
12	Harmony with the surrounding historical context. Incorporation of pitched roofs and wooden arched windows. Use of traditional Iranian materials (bricks and tiles).	■	■	□	■	■
21	Continuity among facades. Use of common materials (stone and brick).	■	■	□	■	■

The data in Table 8.4 indicates that all selected facades adhere to the second principle of Iranian architecture, as they lack extravagant ornamentation. With a single exception, all facades also comply with the structural principle, exhibiting elements of rhythm, proportion, symmetry and modular grid. The materials used in these facades are primarily local and predominantly bricks, in accordance with the principle of self-sufficiency. However, due to changes in contemporary lifestyle, none of the buildings adhere to the principle of introversion, with only the building facade in District 6 exhibiting consideration for privacy. Additionally, designers in some areas have neglected the first principle in their facade designs by failing to account for human scale and coordination within the broader residential environment.

Conclusion

Worthington observes that an effective designer should manage change and adjustment in a way that not only preserves the past, but also adds to our understanding while simultaneously opening up opportunities for the future. This is essential because contexts and monuments need to be used in order to survive.[24]

In architectural design, the treatment of historical buildings and contexts should not be based solely on physical appearance but also on the principles and rules governing historical and traditional architecture. The findings of this research show that the majority of selected facades are comply with the principles of traditional Iranian architecture. Although the study does not include all facades approved by the committees, the selected facades were chosen as exemplary models of the best facades in each district and were presented at a joint meeting of the facade committees.

These facades can serve as models for optimising residential facades in the metropolis of Tehran. Adhering to these principles is an important step towards appropriate and purposeful design, providing a viable framework for future designers. Furthermore, despite the challenges faced by the facade committees in their operations, they have been able to make a positive, albeit modest, contribution to improving the visual quality of Tehran's metropolitan image and creating a promising vision for the future.

Given the aforementioned obstacles, the effective functioning of facade committees depends on close collaboration among relevant experts, designers and citizens. Organising educational classes and

---

24 John Worthington, 'Managing and Moderating Change', in *Context: New Buildings in Historic Settings*, ed. by John Warren, John Worthington and Sue Taylor (York: Architectural Press, 1998), p. 5.

workshops can enable citizens to learn about the principles of facade design. Moreover, enacting legal regulations governing the planning and review stages of the facade design process would help to ensure their visual quality. Achieving all of these objectives necessitates cooperation among designers and citizens to promote awareness and aesthetic literacy across society.

Bibliography

City of Richmond, Department of Urban Planning & Development Review, 'Façade Design Guide' (2013), https://www.rva.gov/sites/default/files/2023-06/PDR%20-%20Aaron%20Bond%20-%20FIP%20Design%20Guide%20FINAL.pdf

Daryani, Mehdi, *The Principles of Facade Design* (Tehran: Avalo Akhar, 2014).

Khodamipoor, Zabihi, Hoessein and Mofidi Shemirani, Seyed Majid, 'Evaluation of Components Influential on Promotion of Landscape Identity of Architecture of Contemporary View', *Journal of Research and Urban Planning*, 4111 (2020), 197–214, https://dorl.net/dor/20.1001.1.22285229.1399.11.41.13.2

Krier, Rob, *Elements of Architecture* (London: Academy Editions, 1992).

Lynch, Kevin, *The Image of the City* (Cambridge, MA: MIT Press, 1960). Madanipour, Ali, 'Tehran, National Capital, Iran' (9 April 2025), *Britannica*, https://www.britannica.com/place/Tehran

Masoudinejad, Sepideh and Aliyas, Zeynab, 'Investigating the Components of Façade Aesthetic and its Effect on Urban Identity', paper presented at the 'International Conference on Civil Engineering, Architecture and Urban Management in Iran' (Tehran, 2017).

Mokhtarpour, Akbar, Heydarian, Simin and Moslehabadi, Fatemeh, *Cityscape, with an Approach to Standards and Principles* (Tehran: Honare-Memari, 2016).Peyvastehgar, Yaghoub, Heidari, Ali Akbar and Eslami, Motahareh, 'Recognition of the Pyrnia's Five Principles in the Iranian Traditional Home and its Analysis Based on Islamic Sources', *Journal of Iranian-Islamic City Studies*, 27 (2017), 51–66.

Pirnya, Mohamad Karim, *Recognition of Iranian Architecture Styles* (Tehran: Soroush Danesh, 2001).Pourdehghan, Hafezeh, Shahcheraghi, Azadeh, Mokhtabad, Seyed Mostafa and Majedi, Hamid, 'Evaluating Visual Preferences of Architect and People toward Housing Facades, Using Multidimensional Scaling Analysis (MDS)', *International Journal of Space Ontology*, 4 (2017), 75–85.

Poordehghan, Hafezeh, Shahcheraghi, Azadeh and Mokhtabad, Seyed Mostafa, 'Evaluation and Analysis of the Theoretical Principles of Describable

Housing According to the Opinions of Citizens', *Journal of Housing and Rural Environment*, 38 (2019), 81–96.

Sadeghi, Alireza, Mousavi, Elaheh, Baghi, Sarvineh and Khodaee, Zahra, 'Utilizing Iranian-Islamic Approach in the Analysis and Improvement Process of the Quality of Urban Facades', *Journal of Iranian Architecture and Urbanism*, 2 (2019), 69–84, https://doi.org/10.30475/isau.2019.87934

Sefatgol, Mansur, 'Rethinking the Safavid Iran', *Journal of Asian and African Studies*, 72 (2006), 5–17.

Worthington, John, 'Managing and Moderating Change', in *Context: New Buildings in Historic Settings*, ed. by John Warren, John Worthington and Sue Taylor (York: Architectural Press, 1998), pp. 3–5.

Zarif Pour Langrodi, Anahita, Alborzi, Fariba and Soheili, Jamalodin, 'Explaining the Role of Urban Views in Creating Placing Attachment for Citizens (Case Study: Tehran Residential Views)', *Journal of Research and Urban Planning*, 20 (2020), 217–32, https://dorl.net/dor/20.1001.1.22285229.1399.11.40.15.2

9. Envelope Impact on the Thermal Performance of a Contemporary Building in Downtown Tunis

Athar Chabchoub and Fakher Kharrat

Introduction

This chapter explores the impact of building envelope composition on indoor thermal comfort. An initial thermal study was conducted using two analytical indices to evaluate the thermal performance of a contemporary corner building in Tunis during August, the hottest month of the year. The results of this assessment made it possible to identify deficiencies in the building's design. Subsequently, a parametric study was carried out through simulations of four envelope scenarios using the TRNSYS (Transient System Simulation Tool) model. This study highlighted the regulatory impact of envelopes with high thermal inertia on indoor thermal comfort in a Mediterranean climate. Thus, with a few remedial actions, it is possible to optimise the thermal performance of contemporary buildings in Tunis.

Across history and throughout the world, humans have adapted architecture to their local climates and surroundings, giving rise to diverse architectural styles specific to each region. However, the emergence of an international style in recent decades has led to the homogenisation of large and medium-sized cities across the globe. This standardisation of contemporary architecture often disregards climate considerations, with significant consequences not only in terms of the quality of buildings and the health and well-being of occupants, but also for the environment.

Climate-conscious design is critical in order for a building to meet its users comfort needs. Thermal comfort, more so than acoustic, visual or olfactory comfort, is essential for indoor quality of life, with thermal appreciation emerging as a response to the influence of climatic factors on a building. However, contemporary architects often prioritise aesthetics over thermal quality, producing buildings poorly adapted to local climates. This results in uncomfortable spaces requiring the intensive use of heating and cooling systems, which create 'artificial' microclimates.

In this context, it is the architect's responsibility to reconcile user requirements with environmental considerations in order to ensure comfortable buildings with interior microclimates conducive to occupants' well-being. This requires a conceptual process based on a thorough understanding of the interactions and thermal exchanges between indoor and outdoor environments.

Acknowledging the fundamental role of architectural choices in optimising buildings' thermal and energy performance, researchers have examined various strategies for enhancing architectural design. These studies have shown that thermal quality is influenced by several parameters, including buildings' shape, density, orientation, solar protection, and construction materials as well as the thermal inertia of their envelopes.[1]

---

1   Shakila Pathirana, Asanka Rodrigo and Rangika Halwatura, 'Effect of Building Shape, Orientation, Window to Wall Ratios and Zones on Energy Efficiency and Thermal Comfort of Naturally Ventilated Houses in Tropical Climate', *International Journal of Energy and Environment Engineering*, 10 (2019), 107–20; Aiman Albatayneh, Dariusz Alterman, Adrian Page and Behdaad Moghtaderi, 'The Significance of the Orientation on the Overall Buildings Thermal Performance—Case Study in Australia', *Energy Procedia*, 152 (2018), 372–77; Laura Bellia, Marino Concetta, Francesco Minichiello and Alessia Pedace, 'An Overview on Solar Shading Systems for Buildings', *Energy Procedia*, 62 (2014), 309–17; Rania Elghamry and Hamdy Hassan, 'Impact of Window Parameters on the Building Envelope on the Thermal Comfort, Energy Consumption and Cost and Environment', *International Journal of Ventilation*, 19.4 (2020), 233–59;

Among these parameters, envelope composition remains the most influential. Accordingly, this research seeks to understand how the envelope of a contemporary building in Tunis can impact its thermal performance, in order to uncover solutions to the problems posed by the maladaptation of contemporary architecture to local climates.

Conceptualising Indoor Thermal Comfort

The concept of indoor thermal comfort is more challenging to define than it may at first appear. From the abundant theorising and numerous studies on the subject, three distinct definitional perspectives emerge:

1. The physiological perspective: Baruch Givoni[2] and Jean Baptiste Hoffmann[3] argue that the essential parameters defining overall thermal comfort are related not to the environment but to the body.

2. The psychological perspective: According to the regulations of the American Society of Heating, Refrigerating and AirConditioning Engineers (ASHRAE)[4] and the Association Française de Normalisation (AFNOR) [the French standardisation association],[5] comfort is defined as a state of mind characterised by satisfaction with the thermal environment.

Pooya Lotfabadi and Polat Hançer Polat, 'Comparative Study of Traditional and Contemporary Building Envelope Construction Techniques in Terms of Thermal Comfort and Energy Efficiency in Hot and Humid Climates', *Sustainability*, 11.13:3582 (2019); Raad Homod, Amjad Almusaed, Assad Almssad, Manar Jaafar, Marjan Goodarzi and Khairul Sahari, 'Effect of Different Building Envelope Materials on Thermal Comfort and Air-Conditioning Energy Savings: A Case Study in Basra City, Iraq', *Journal of Energy Storage*, 101975 (2020).

2   Baruch Givoni, *Climate Consideration in Building and Urban Design* (New York: John Wiley & Sons Inc., 1998).

3   Jean-Baptiste Hoffmann, 'Ambiances climatiques et confort thermique', Proceedings of COSTIC, Saint-Rémy-lès-Chevreuse, France (1994).

4   ASHRAE, *Handbook of Fundamentals* (Atlanta, GA: SI Edition, 1997).

5   AFNOR, *Ambiances thermiques modérées—Détermination des indices PMV et PPD et spécification des conditions de confort thermique, Norme NF EN ISO 7730* (Paris: AFNOR Editions, 1995).

3. The physical perspective: P. O. Fanger [6] and Patrick Depecker and colleagues[7] assert that a comfortable environment is one in which the human organism can maintain a constant temperature without perceptively activating instinctive thermoregulatory mechanisms against heat and cold.

The unique habits, moods, perceptions and behaviours of each individual give rise to differences in thermal sensations. Thus, it can be said that the three aspects of thermal comfort espoused by these perspectives are strongly linked. However, continuous technological advances and upheavals produce new problems as well as solutions when it comes to comfort. With the increasingly materialistic associations of modern comfort,[8] thermal comfort is thus distorted by the excessive use of air conditioning systems. This attests to the maladaptation of new constructions to local climates, privileging aesthetics over comfort.

Methodology

Designing comfortable buildings not only benefits the environment by reducing energy consumption but also has a positive impact on the well-being and health of occupants. This can only be achieved by tailoring buildings to their local climate.

With the aim of deepening knowledge on the complexities of 'building–climate' interaction in order to optimise buildings' thermal performance, our study utilises two approaches. The first of these, the analytical approach, seeks to evaluate the thermal performance of a contemporary building in Tunis. The second, the parametric approach, applies different scenarios of envelope composition to shed light on how this factor impacts thermal comfort.

The study focuses on a contemporary corner building located in the colonial fabric of downtown Tunis, specifically in the Lafayette District.

---

6   P. O. Fanger, *Thermal Comfort* (Copenhagen: Danish Technical Press, 1970); P.O. Fanger and J. Tofum, 'Extension of the PMV Model to Non-air-conditioned Buildings in Warm Climates', *Energy and Buildings*, 34.6 (2002), 533–36.

7   Patrick Depecker *et al.*, *Qualité thermique des ambiances*, Collection cahiers pédagogiques thermique et architecture (Paris: AFME, 1989).

8   Jean-Pierre Goubert, *Du luxe au confort* (Paris: Edition Belin, 1988).

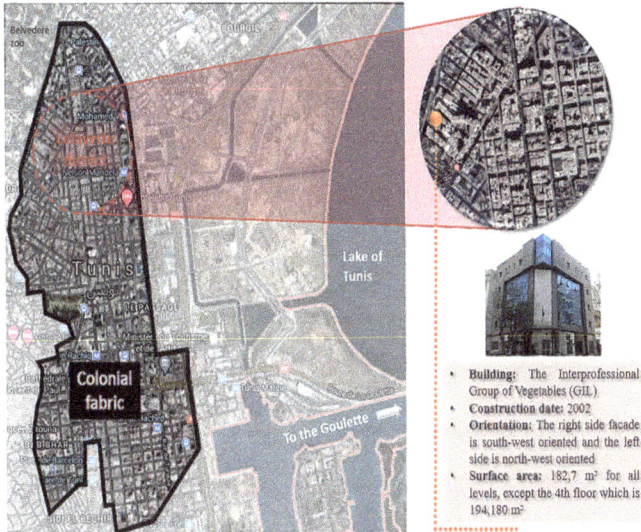

This four-storey office building, with a facade glazing percentage of 49.48%, was constructed using a contemporary building system, as detailed in the table below.

Table 9.1 Construction techniques and materials used for the floors and the walls of the studied building. Author's illustrations, 2021, CC BY-NC-ND.

Common floor (including ground floor, 1st, 2nd, 3rd and 4th floors), thickness = 30 cm	
	1. Granito-marbled tiles 2. Laying mortar 3. Laying sand 4. Compression screed (5 cm) 5. Hollow clay brick (16 cm) 6. Ceiling plaster (cement)
Terrace floor (thickness = 40 cm)	
	1. Sealing 2. Slope in lean concrete (250 kg/m³) 3. Compression screed (5 cm) 4. Hollow clay brick (16 cm) 5. Ceiling plaster (cement)

Facade walls (double partition wall, thickness = 35 cm)		
Outside	Inside	1. Coating 2. Hollow clay brick 3. Air blade 4. Hollow clay brick 5. Cement plaster

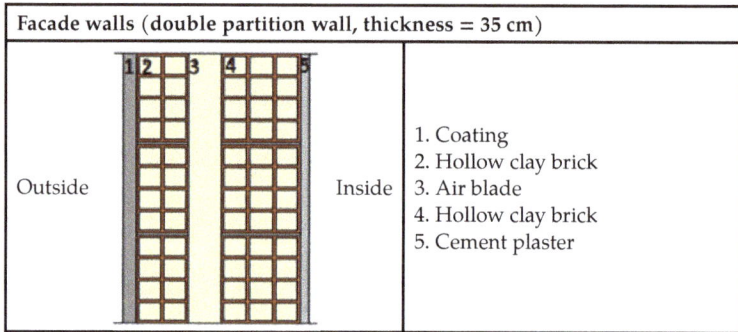

The research was conducted during the month of August, selected on the basis of survey feedback from occupants of buildings in downtown Tunis, who reported feeling greater discomfort due to high summer temperatures than to the winter cold.

Analytical Approach

A person's thermal comfort depends first on their environment and then on their bodily reactions, responses and sensations. In this section, we focus on evaluating thermal performance through two analytical indices: Predicted Mean Vote (PMV)[9] and Standard Effective Temperature (SET).[10] Calculating these indices entails considering how users interact with their environment, taking into account data gathered through in-situ observation on activity level (metabolic rate) and clothing insulation.

Given that the structure under study is an office building, the metabolic rate was calculated according to ISO 8996 for sedentary subjects engaged in computer work. Two categories of clothing insulation were identified based on our observations, representing two typical summer outfits.

9   ISO, *Ergonomics of the Thermal Environment—Analytical Determination and Interpretation of Thermal Comfort Using Calculation of the PMV and PPD Indices and Local Thermal Comfort Criteria*, ISO 7730, 3rd edn (2005), https://cdn.standards.iteh.ai/samples/39155/9632a0563ca742209edb45856ff69296/ISO-7730-2005.pdf
10   A. Pharo Gagge *et al.*, 'A Standard Predictive Index of Human Response to the Thermal Environment', *ASHRAE Transactions*, 92 (1986), 86–114.

Table 9.2 Description of typical outfits.

Outfit A: Light summer outfit		Outfit B: Light work clothes (summer)	
Clothes	Clo	Clothes	Clo
Underwear	0.03	Underwear	0.03
Light pants	0.26	Moderate pants (for work)	0.32
Lightweight, short-sleeved shirt	0.14	Lightweight long-sleeved shirt	0.22
Sandals	0.02	Shoes (moccasin type)	0.04
Total	**0.45**	**Total**	**0.62**

Evaluation of Indoor Thermal Comfort through the PMV Index

The thermal evaluation using the PMV index was based on numerical simulations made with the TRNSYS model. The building was then classified into distinct thermal zones in order to analyse each area's thermal behaviour in relation to its orientation (i.e., whether it faces the street, courtyard, etc.).

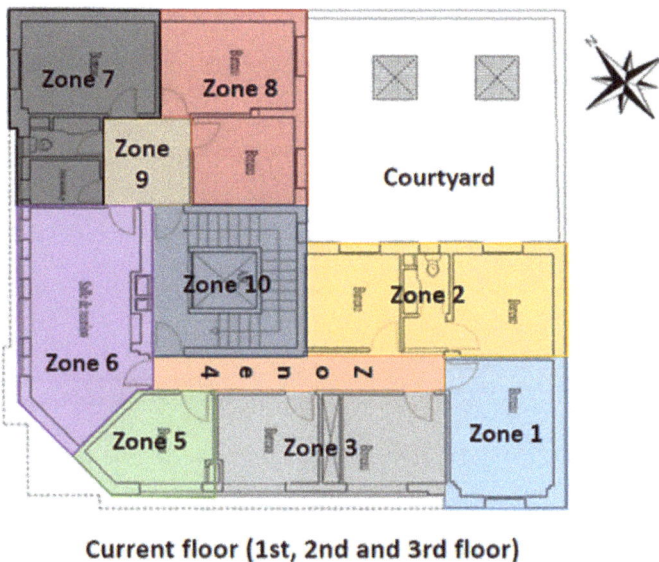

Current floor (1st, 2nd and 3rd floor)

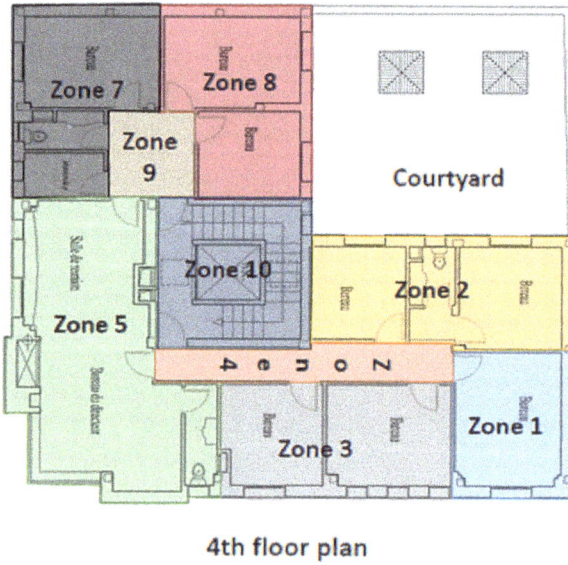

4th floor plan

Fig. 9.2 Thermal division of the studied building (scale 1/200). Author's illustration, CC BY-NC-ND.

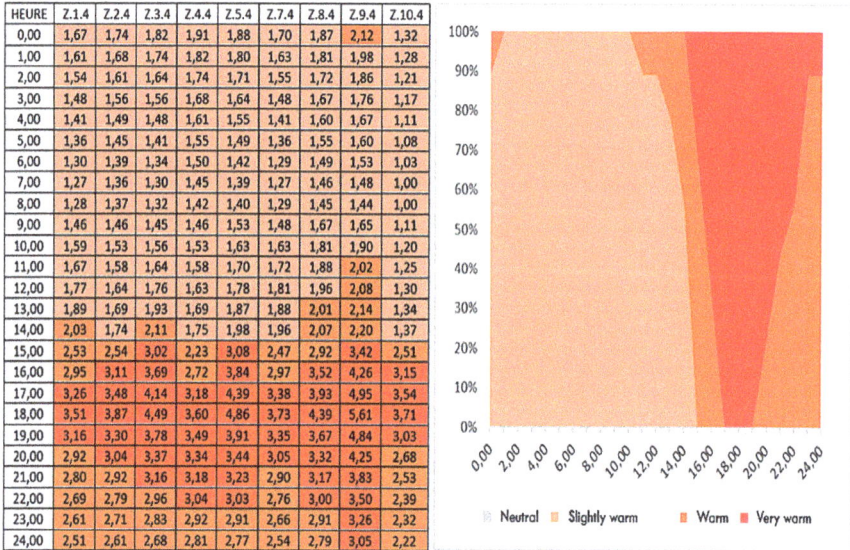

HEURE	Z.1.4	Z.2.4	Z.3.4	Z.4.4	Z.5.4	Z.7.4	Z.8.4	Z.9.4	Z.10.4
0,00	1,67	1,74	1,82	1,91	1,88	1,70	1,87	2,12	1,32
1,00	1,61	1,68	1,74	1,82	1,80	1,63	1,81	1,98	1,28
2,00	1,54	1,61	1,64	1,74	1,71	1,55	1,72	1,86	1,21
3,00	1,48	1,56	1,56	1,68	1,64	1,48	1,67	1,76	1,17
4,00	1,41	1,49	1,48	1,61	1,55	1,41	1,60	1,67	1,11
5,00	1,36	1,45	1,41	1,55	1,49	1,36	1,55	1,60	1,08
6,00	1,30	1,39	1,34	1,50	1,42	1,29	1,49	1,53	1,03
7,00	1,27	1,36	1,30	1,45	1,39	1,27	1,46	1,48	1,00
8,00	1,28	1,37	1,32	1,42	1,40	1,29	1,45	1,44	1,00
9,00	1,46	1,46	1,45	1,46	1,53	1,48	1,67	1,65	1,11
10,00	1,59	1,53	1,56	1,53	1,63	1,63	1,81	1,90	1,20
11,00	1,67	1,58	1,64	1,58	1,70	1,72	1,88	2,02	1,25
12,00	1,77	1,64	1,76	1,63	1,78	1,81	1,96	2,08	1,30
13,00	1,89	1,69	1,93	1,69	1,87	1,88	2,01	2,14	1,34
14,00	2,03	1,74	2,11	1,75	1,98	1,96	2,07	2,20	1,37
15,00	2,53	2,54	3,02	2,23	3,08	2,47	2,92	3,42	2,51
16,00	2,95	3,11	3,69	2,72	3,84	2,97	3,52	4,26	3,15
17,00	3,26	3,48	4,14	3,18	4,39	3,38	3,93	4,95	3,54
18,00	3,51	3,87	4,49	3,60	4,86	3,73	4,39	5,61	3,71
19,00	3,16	3,30	3,78	3,49	3,91	3,35	3,67	4,84	3,03
20,00	2,92	3,04	3,37	3,34	3,44	3,05	3,32	4,25	2,68
21,00	2,80	2,92	3,16	3,18	3,23	2,90	3,17	3,83	2,53
22,00	2,69	2,79	2,96	3,04	3,03	2,76	3,00	3,50	2,39
23,00	2,61	2,71	2,83	2,92	2,91	2,66	2,91	3,26	2,32
24,00	2,51	2,61	2,68	2,81	2,77	2,54	2,79	3,05	2,22

Neutral   Slightly warm   Warm   Very warm

Fig. 9.3 Daily variations in PMV on the fourth floor of the studied building. Heure = hour; Z = zone. Author's graph, CC BY-NC-ND.

From the simulations conducted, we first established the PMV variations throughout each day during the month of August, across all thermal zones and different floors. This allowed us to develop a graphical illustration of comfort zone distribution over time (Figure 9.3). After analysing the daily variations in different zones over thirty days, we calculated the daily averages for each thermal zone across the four floors of the building (Figure 9.4).

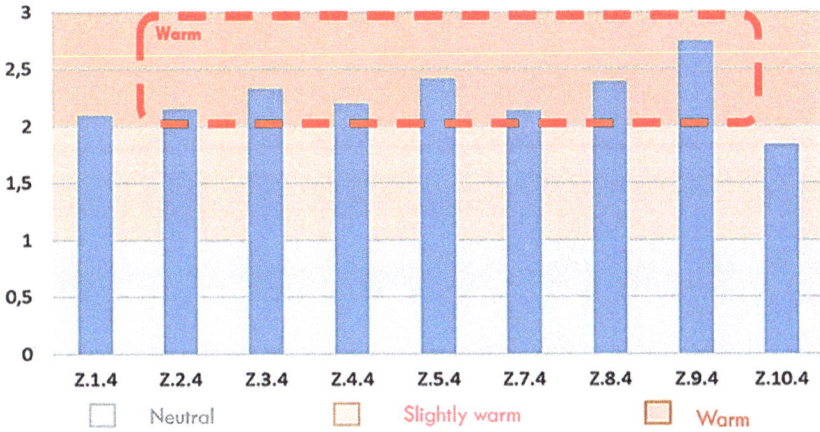

Fig. 9.4 Daily averages of PMV on the fourth floor of the studied building. Z = zone. Author's graph, CC BY-NC-ND.

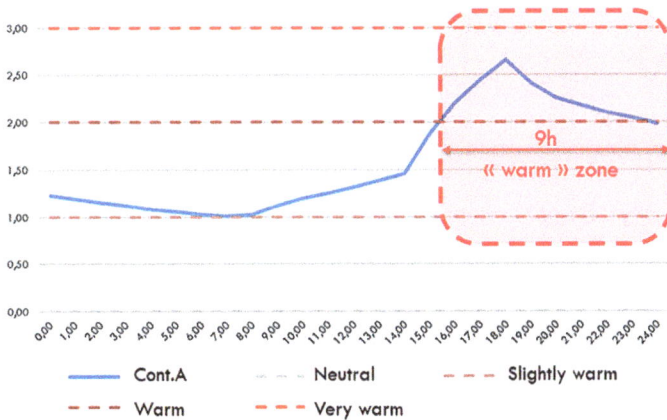

Fig. 9.5 Average daily variations in PMV (for August). X axis = time of day (h); Y axis = PMV; Cont.A = Contemporary building A. Author's graph, CC BY-NC-ND.

From these averages in Figure 9.4, we were able to obtain the PMV value of the entire building, which was 1.59. According to the thermal sensation scale provided by ASHRAE, the building qualifies as 'slightly warm' to 'warm'. More specifically, the overall average daily PMV variations throughout the month of August (Figure 9.5) indicate that the building spends fifteen hours in the 'slightly warm' zone and nine hours in the 'warm' zone.

Evaluation of Indoor Thermal Comfort through the SET Index

To navigate the complexity of calculating the Standard Effective Temperature (SET) index, which requires very precise information such as skin wettedness, we used the Center for the Built Environment (CBE) Thermal Comfort Tool proposed by ASHRAE. Upon inputting the microclimatic data obtained from the simulations—specifically air temperature (Ta), mean radiant temperature (Tmrt) and relative humidity (HR)—into the calculation tool, we obtained the SET index values and proceeded to analyse the variations and daily averages across all zones and floors.

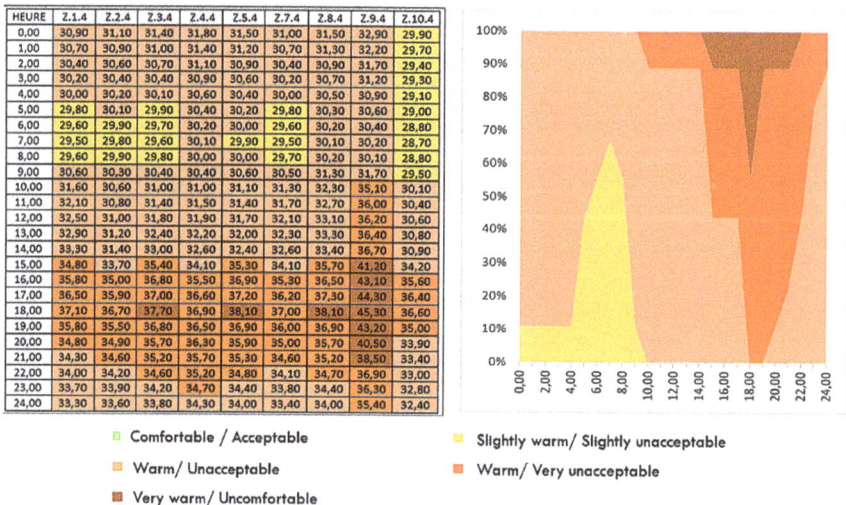

HEURE	Z.1.4	Z.2.4	Z.3.4	Z.4.4	Z.5.4	Z.7.4	Z.8.4	Z.9.4	Z.10.4
0,00	30,90	31,10	31,40	31,80	31,50	31,00	31,50	32,90	29,90
1,00	30,70	30,90	31,00	31,40	31,20	30,70	31,30	32,20	29,70
2,00	30,40	30,60	30,70	31,10	30,90	30,40	30,90	31,70	29,40
3,00	30,20	30,40	30,40	30,90	30,60	30,20	30,70	31,20	29,30
4,00	30,00	30,20	30,10	30,60	30,40	30,00	30,50	30,90	29,10
5,00	29,80	30,10	29,90	30,40	30,20	29,80	30,30	30,60	29,00
6,00	29,60	29,90	29,70	30,20	30,00	29,60	30,20	30,40	28,80
7,00	29,50	29,80	29,60	30,10	29,90	29,50	30,10	30,20	28,70
8,00	29,60	29,90	29,80	30,00	30,00	29,70	30,20	30,10	28,80
9,00	30,60	30,30	30,40	30,40	30,60	30,50	31,30	31,70	29,50
10,00	31,60	30,60	31,00	31,00	31,10	31,30	32,30	35,10	30,10
11,00	32,10	30,80	31,40	31,50	31,40	31,70	32,70	36,00	29,40
12,00	32,50	31,00	31,80	31,90	31,70	32,10	33,10	36,20	30,60
13,00	32,90	31,20	32,40	32,20	32,00	32,30	33,30	36,40	30,80
14,00	33,30	31,40	33,00	32,60	32,40	32,60	33,40	36,70	30,90
15,00	34,80	33,70	35,40	34,10	35,30	34,10	35,70	41,20	34,20
16,00	35,80	35,00	36,80	35,50	36,90	35,30	36,50	43,10	35,60
17,00	36,50	35,90	37,00	36,60	37,20	36,20	37,30	44,30	36,40
18,00	37,10	36,70	37,70	36,90	38,10	37,00	38,10	45,30	36,60
19,00	35,80	35,50	36,80	36,50	36,90	36,00	36,90	43,20	35,00
20,00	34,80	34,90	35,70	36,30	35,90	35,00	35,70	40,50	33,90
21,00	34,30	34,60	35,20	35,70	35,30	34,60	35,20	38,50	33,40
22,00	34,00	34,20	34,60	35,20	34,80	34,10	34,70	36,90	33,00
23,00	33,70	33,90	34,20	34,70	34,40	33,80	34,40	36,30	32,80
24,00	33,30	33,60	33,80	34,30	34,00	33,40	34,00	35,40	32,40

Legend:
- ☐ Comfortable / Acceptable
- ☐ Slightly warm/ Slightly unacceptable
- ☐ Warm/ Unacceptable
- ☐ Warm/ Very unacceptable
- ☐ Very warm/ Uncomfortable

Fig. 9.6 Daily variations of the SET at the level of the fourth floor of the studied building. Heure = hour; Z = zone. Author's graph, CC BY-NC-ND.

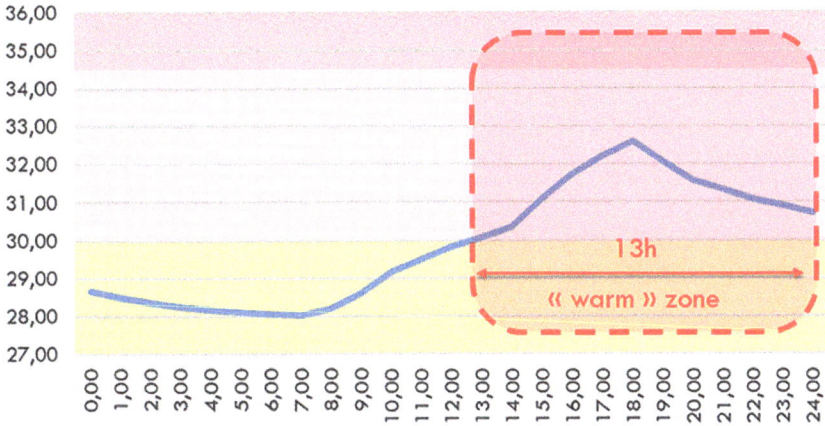

Fig. 9.7 Average daily variations in SET (for August). X axis = time of day (h); Y axis = SET; Author's graph, CC BY-NC-ND.

Following the same procedure used to evaluate the PMV index, we determined that the overall SET index value of the studied building is 30.79°C, corresponding to the thermal sensation categories of 'warm', 'unacceptable' and 'uncomfortable'. Referencing the above graph of daily averages, it is evident that the building spends thirteen hours in the 'warm-unacceptable' zone and eleven hours in the 'slightly warm' zone.

Parametric Approach

Given the substantial amount of time the building spends in the 'hot' zone according to the PMV and SET evaluations, an architectural intervention is needed to remedy the thermal deficiencies of this building and improve future constructions. To this end, we carried out a parametric study to discern the impact of envelope materials on the thermal quality of the building. Subsequently, we focused on two cases and tested two scenarios for each.

- Case 1: rubble stone walls
  - Scenario 1: use of a solid brick floor over vaults (colonial-era construction technique)
  - Scenario 2: use of a hollow brick floor (contemporary construction technique)

- Case 2: solid brick walls

  o Scenario 1: use of a solid brick floor over vaults (colonial-era construction technique)

  o Scenario 2: use of a hollow brick floor (contemporary construction technique)

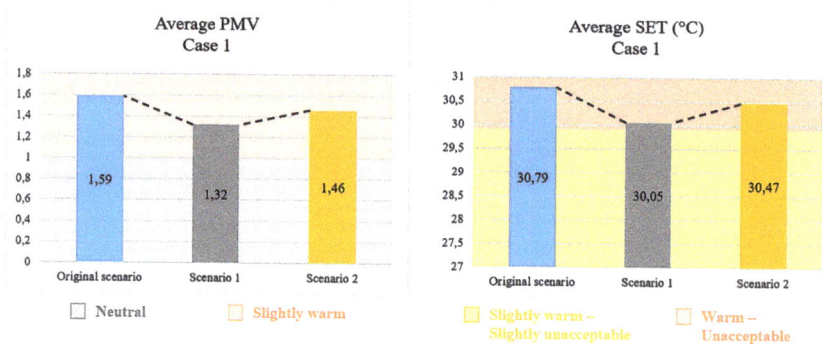

Fig. 9.8 Evaluation of thermal comfort through PMV and SET for the two scenarios in Case 1. Author's graphs, CC BY-NC-ND.

The results indicate that all four scenarios studied (two scenarios for each case) made it possible to improve the building's thermal response. Therefore, envelope materials can be concluded to play an important role in optimising the performance of buildings.

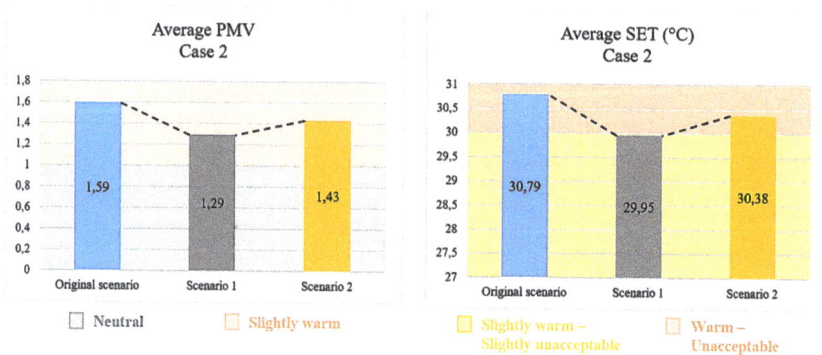

Fig. 9.9 Evaluation of thermal comfort through PMV and SET for the two scenarios in Case 2. Author's graphs, CC BY-NC-ND.

Results

The results of altering the composition of the building envelope, summarised in Table 9.3, indicate that all four scenarios examined have the potential to enhance the thermal performance of the building. However, the most efficient envelope is that of Case 2, Scenario 1, with solid brick walls and vaulted floors. In addition to thermal improvement, this envelope reduced the hours spent in 'hot' zones to seven hours based on PMV and five hours based on SET. Meanwhile, the performance of the configuration in Case 1, Scenario 2 (rubble stone wall with solid brick flooring over vaults) is closely comparable to the envelope of Case 2, Scenario 1.

Table 9.3 Summary of the results of the parametric study. S W = Slightly Warm; W-U = Warm-Unacceptable.

			PMV	Number of hours in 'Warm' zone (compared to PMV)	SET (°C)	Number of hours in 'Warm-Unacceptable' zone (compared to SET)
Original			1.59 S W	9 hours	30.79 W-U	15 hours
Envelope composition	Rubble	Scenario 1: Floor on vaults	1.32 S W	2 hours	30.05 W-U	11 hours
		Scenario 2: Hollow brick floor	1.46 S W	4 hours	30.47 W-U	12 hours
	Solid brick	Scenario 1: Floor on vaults	1.29 S W	almost 2 hours	29.95 W-U	10 hours
		Scenario 2: Hollow brick floor	1.43 S W	4 hours	30.38 W-U	11 hours and 30 minutes

Thus, while envelopes with high thermal inertia (Case 1, Scenario 1 and Case 2, Scenario 1) may be more judicious, especially considering the high summer temperatures in Tunis, contemporary flooring constructions paired with walls with high thermal inertia (Case 1, Scenario 2 and Case 2, Scenario 2) are also a viable solution. Not only do they optimise thermal performance, but they save time during construction due to the ease of installing contemporary floors.

Conclusion

Given its significant energy and environmental implications, the thermal comfort of indoor spaces is a critical concern in the building sector today. Accordingly, this chapter highlights the importance of the physical properties of construction materials, calling for particular attention to the composition of building envelopes during architectural design. This feature can have a direct impact on occupants' thermal well-being as well as an indirect impact on the environment, reducing energy consumption in response to thermal discomfort.

Additionally, with the objective of improving the thermal quality of contemporary buildings in Tunis, this study demonstrates that heavy and compact materials with high thermal inertia are best suited to the local climate. These materials mitigate discomfort caused by outdoor temperature variations, particularly in summer. Thus, addressing the issue of inappropriate material choices in the construction of contemporary building envelopes in Tunis, this research contributes to resolving the thermal, energy and environmental problems associated with modern designs through corrective measures within contemporary construction systems.

Bibliography

AFNOR, *Ambiances thermiques modérées—Détermination des indices PMV et PPD et spécification des conditions de confort thermique, Norme NF EN ISO 7730* (Paris: AFNOR Editions, 1995).

Albatayneh, Aiman, Alterman, Dariusz, Page, Adrian and Moghtaderi, Behdaad, 'The Significance of the Orientation on the Overall Buildings Thermal Performance—Case Study in Australia', *Energy Procedia*, 152 (2018), 372–77, https://doi.org/10.1016/j.egypro.2018.09.159

ASHRAE, *Handbook of Fundamentals* (Atlanta, GA: SI Edition, 1997).

Bellia, Laura, Concetta, Marino, Minichiello, Francesco and Pedace, Alessia, 'An Overview on Solar Shading Systems for Buildings', *Energy Procedia*, 62 (2014), 309–17, https://doi.org/10.1016/j.egypro.2014.12.392

Depecker, Patrick, *et al.*, *Qualité thermique des ambiances*, Collection cahiers pédagogiques thermique et architecture (Paris: AFME, 1989).

Elghamry, Rania and Hassan, Hamdy, 'Impact of Window Parameters on the Building Envelope on the Thermal Comfort, Energy Consumption and Cost and Environment', *International Journal of Ventilation*, 19.4 (2020), 233–59, https://doi.org/10.1080/14733315.2019.1665784

Fanger, P. O., *Thermal Comfort* (Copenhagen: Danish Technical Press, 1970).

Fanger, P. O., and Tofum, J., 'Extension of the PMV Model to Non-air-conditioned Buildings in Warm Climates', *Energy and Buildings*, 34.6 (2002), 533–36. Givoni, Baruch, *Climate Consideration in Building and Urban Design* (New York: John Wiley & Sons Inc., 1998).

Goubert, J.-P., *Du luxe au confort* (Paris: Edition Belin, 1988).

Hoffmann, Jean-Baptiste, 'Ambiances climatiques et confort thermique', Proceedings of COSTIC, Saint-Rémy-lès-Chevreuse, France (1994).

Homod, Raad, Almusaed, Amjad, Almssad, Assad, Jaafar, Manar, Goodarzi, Marjan and Sahari, Khairul, 'Effect of Different Building Envelope Materials on Thermal Comfort and Air-Conditioning Energy Savings: A Case Study in Basra City, Iraq', *Journal of Energy Storage*, 101975 (2020), https://doi.org/10.1016/j.est.2020.101975

ISO, *Ergonomics of the Thermal Environment—Analytical Determination and Interpretation of Thermal Comfort Using Calculation of the PMV and PPD Indices and Local Thermal Comfort Criteria*, ISO 7730, 3rd edn (2005), https://cdn.standards.iteh.ai/samples/39155/9632a0563ca742209edb45856ff69296/ISO-7730-2005.pdf

Lotfabadi, Pooya and Hançer, Polat, 'Comparative Study of Traditional and Contemporary Building Envelope Construction Techniques in Terms of Thermal Comfort and Energy Efficiency in Hot and Humid Climates', *Sustainability*, 11.13:3582 (2019), https://doi.org/10.3390/su11133582

Pharo Gagge, A. *et al.*, 'A Standard Predictive Index of Human Response to the Thermal Environment', *ASHRAE Transactions*, 92 (1986), 86–114.

Remon L., 'The Effect of Building Geometric Shape and Orientation on its Energy Performance in Various Climate Regions', *International Journal of GEOMATE*, 16.53 (2019), 113–19.

Shakila, Pathirana, Rodrigo, Asanka and Halwatura, Rangika, 'Effect of Building Shape, Orientation, Window to Wall Ratios and Zones on Energy Efficiency and Thermal Comfort of Naturally Ventilated Houses in Tropical Climate', *International Journal of Energy and Environment Engineering*, 10 (2019), 107–20, https://doi.org/10.1007/s40095-018-0295-3

Conclusion

Housing in the Global Context of Urbanisation

Lilia Makhloufi

This book has highlighted different case studies analysed by researchers and practitioners from different backgrounds and countries. The contributors, spanning architects, archaeologists, urban sociologists, urban designers, urban planners and landscape architects, examined local heritage and housing over time—from past to present—while discussing cultural challenges and opportunities. Their analyses of past housing conditions aimed to inform contemporary and future practices.

In this book, priority was given to interdisciplinary perspectives on modern residential buildings and the principles used today in contemporary cities in Syria, Morocco, Egypt, Iran and Tunisia. The contributors did not approach architectural and urban processes as independent from their social contexts, but rather as intricately intertwined with them. In this context, architects emphasised the sustainability of buildings, particularly their facades and envelopes.

Today, in light of rapid urbanisation, repetitive architecture seems unavoidable, resulting from the prefabrication processes employed by property developers all around the world. This rapid urbanisation has led to the global standardisation of architectural and urban production, at the expense of representing local identities and cultures. However, for most people, the images evoked by their home and town are inextricably linked to the processes of identity development. Moreover, perceptions

 https://doi.org/10.11647/OBP.0460.10

of housing are deeply connected to how it is used by residents from the moment they move in, whether dictated by choice or circumstance. Therefore, successful urban planning must consider urban character while also respecting local identity.

This interdisciplinary book emphasises that residents' representations of their residential spaces depend closely on their experiences—personal, social and spatial. Furthermore, when constrained by user attitudes, cities cannot be conceived independently of their contexts. They must be defined according to the will and prerogatives of local actors as well as, crucially, inhabitants' needs.

The goal of sustainable urban development is to enable all people to satisfy their basic needs, while enhancing their quality of life without compromising the well-being of future generations. Sustainable development also encompasses human development, values and cultures. Here, sustainable human development highlights the importance of housing quality and inclusive decision-making processes.

Metropolises today are characterised by high population density, considerable urban development and a multitude of bordering districts with an abundance of residential spaces. These have been facilitated by the increased mobility of capital and technological progress as well as reductions in costs associated with transportation and data processing.

In the process of urbanisation, particular importance has been placed on public facilities and infrastructures. Urban planners often endeavour to adhere to a general plan in order to achieve harmony among various districts, architectural forms and dwellings, centred around an attractive and modern core. The involvement of the local population is thus imperative when addressing environmental issues and adopting solutions for future residential spaces.

The construction, design and type of housing are critical to the long-term quality of life for inhabitants, who will live in similar architectural and urban spaces. Therefore, greater efforts must be made to increase inhabitants' participation in all stages of the development process, from devising initial plans to handing over keys and beyond. When residents feel a sense of belonging within the housing project and are empowered to contribute to decisions affecting their lives and those of their children, friends and neighbours, the metropolis at large—and its residential spaces in particular—will become more sustainable.

Furthermore, to ensure the long-term liveability of cities for present and future generations, best practices are needed to improve social, economic and environmental conditions. This requires a broader view of inhabitant welfare, an awareness of the consequences of current actions by local decision-makers, and the full involvement of civil society in reaching viable solutions.

Index

About the Team

Alessandra Tosi was the managing editor for this book.

Monica Hanson-Green performed the copy-editing.

Adèle Kreager proof-read this manuscript. Lucy Barnes compiled the index.

The authors created the Alt-text.

Jeevanjot Kaur Nagpal designed the cover. The cover was produced in InDesign using the Fontin font.

Annie Hine typeset the book in InDesign. The main text font is Tex Gyre Pagella and the heading font is Californian FB.

Jeremy Bowman produced the PDF, paperback and hardback editions and created the EPUB.

The conversion to the HTML edition was performed with epublius, an open-source software which is freely available on our GitHub page at https://github.com/OpenBookPublishers

Laura Rodríguez was in charge of marketing.

This book was peer-reviewed by two anonymous referees. Experts in their field, these readers give their time freely to help ensure the academic rigour of our books. We are grateful for their generous and invaluable contributions.

This book need not end here...

Share

All our books — including the one you have just read — are free to access online so that students, researchers and members of the public who can't afford a printed edition will have access to the same ideas. This title will be accessed online by hundreds of readers each month across the globe: why not share the link so that someone you know is one of them?

This book and additional content is available at
https://doi.org/10.11647/OBP.0460

Donate

Open Book Publishers is an award-winning, scholar-led, not-for-profit press making knowledge freely available one book at a time. We don't charge authors to publish with us: instead, our work is supported by our library members and by donations from people who believe that research shouldn't be locked behind paywalls.

Join the effort to free knowledge by supporting us at
https://www.openbookpublishers.com/support-us

We invite you to connect with us on our socials!

BLUESKY	MASTODON	LINKEDIN
@openbookpublish	@OpenBookPublish	open-book-publishers
.bsky.social	@hcommons.social	

Read more at the Open Book Publishers Blog
https://blogs.openbookpublishers.com

You may also be interested in:

Tangible and Intangible Heritage in the Age of Globalisation

Lilia Makhloufi (editor)

https://doi.org/10.11647/OBP.0388

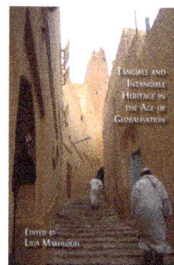

Urban Heritage and Sustainability in the Age of Globalisation

Lilia Makhloufi (editor)

https://doi.org/10.11647/OBP.0412

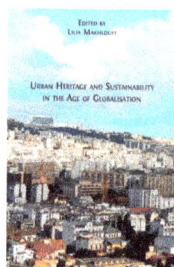

Cultural Heritage Ethics
Between Theory and Practice

Constantine Sandis (editor)

https://doi.org/10.11647/OBP.0047